Vegetarian

Vegetarian

Over 200 healthy recipes

DUMONT
monte

© 2001 DuMont Buchverlag, Köln
Dumont monte, UK, London
All rights reserved
Texts and photographs: Twin Books, Munich, Germany
Printing: Rasch, Bramsche
Binding: Bramscher Buchbinder Betriebe

ISBN 3-7701-7083-0

Printed in Germany

Contents

Introduction

Enjoying food with a clear conscience

It would be possible for us to live on nothing but pills and vitamin drops. But why should we deprive ourselves of the pleasure and enjoyment of looking at and tasting food? Can there be anyone whose heart does not skip a beat in sheer anticipation at the sight of a dish of sumptuous fruit, or a plate of steaming pasta? What could be more pleasant than to sit at a decoratively laid table, in congenial company, and to eat a lovingly prepared meal? We live in a country where we can buy practically all the culinary treasures the world has to offer - vegetables and spices from Asia, fruit from Africa, New Zealand, and South America, wines from Europe and Australia, not forgetting the wonderful variety of garden produce from Europe. We are able to buy all these foreign delicacies thanks to sophisticated refrigeration techniques and a transportation system that spans the entire globe.

Despite the wealth of produce available, the edge has been well and truly taken off our appetite as a result of excessively high levels of hormones in meat, the cattle disease BSE, foot and mouth disease in pigs, sheep, and goats, salmonella in poultry, parasites in fish, and unappetizing ingredients in sausages that pose a health risk. Even those farmers and livestock breeders who are seriously committed to stringent biological methods are unable to give a 100 percent guarantee that their products are completely safe, and so for this reason we are excluding meat, poultry, and fish dishes from the scope of this book.

What do we need?

Energy! Nothing can function without an energy supply. Without gas, your car stays in the garage; without electricity, the train cannot leave the station. Humans are also dependent on an external energy supply - we cannot exist without the energy provided by our daily diet. The most important nutrients that keep us in working order are carbohydrates, protein, and fat. But something crucial is missing from these, namely vitamins and minerals. Although they do not provide energy, without vitamins and minerals our metabolism would not function properly. We would have no protection against diseases, and we would not have strong bones and teeth, nor healthy nerves and muscles.

It is possible to eat your way to good health

Unfortunately, many people nowadays are not very knowledgeable about healthy eating. They believe that all they need to do to stay healthy is to eat an apple a day, or a helping of salad or vegetables. If we consider that most of the diseases to which we are susceptible are the result of poor nutrition, then we should all make it our duty to learn more about nutrition for maintaining good health. Poor nutrition means eating too much or too little, eating too much fat, too much sugar, too much salt, too much protein, and drinking too much alcohol.

Of course, no foodstuffs actually make us ill, but if the body is deficient in particular substances over a prolonged period, then malfunctions occur. The German

few nutrients, or in some cases none at all. These include sugar, alcohol, and white flour products (for this reason it is better to buy wholegrain products). No one wants to forbid particular foods, and you can by all means treat yourself to a slice of pizza, a chocolate bar, or a slice of cake or pie. But always make sure that you eat 200 grams (about 7 ounces) of fruit and 300 grams (10 ounces) of vegetables every day.

Carbohydrates satisfy your hunger

Carbohydrates, found in foods rich in starch and fiber, such as baked potatoes, wholegrain cereals, wholemeal bread and other bakery products, pasta, granola, hulled rice, legumes, vegetables, berries, and bananas are satisfying and keep hunger pangs at bay. Well over half of our daily nutritional needs should be met by products with a high carbohydrate content. High-carbohydrate candies, cakes, cookies, and sodas should be consumed only occasionally due to their low concentration of nutrients. Wholemeal bread accompanied by a little butter, cheese, fruit, or vegetables is more satisfying and supplies many vital nutrients.

Protein for body and mind

The human body needs a daily supply of protein, which is found in food of both animal and vegetable origin. The protein we eat is broken down into amino acids and converted into the body's own protein. Amino acids that the body itself is unable to produce, which are known as essential amino acids, must be supplied from our diet. Approximately 15 percent of our caloric intake should consist of protein. A combination of animal and vegetable proteins is particularly beneficial for the human body, and for this reason combinations such as the following are recommended:

Society for Nutrition (Deutsche Gesellschaft für Ernährung) recommends that cereals and cereal products such as bread and pasta, vegetables, salad, herbs, and fresh fruit should be eaten every day. At least 1 1/2 to 2 liters (approximately 3 to 4 pints/1 1/2 to 2 quarts) of water, herbal tea, or juiced fruit or vegetables should be drunk every day. Milk and milk products such as cheese, yogurt, quark, etc. should form part of the daily diet, but in small quantities; meat, fish, and eggs can all be eaten twice a week. Oils and fats should be used in moderation. Cold pressed oils are preferable to refined culinary oils.

In addition to those foods that are rich in nutrients, however, there is a range of products containing very

is easily disguised. People trying to follow a low-fat diet often do without sandwiches, and reach instead for a chocolate bar or granola bar containing large amounts of fat and sugar. Fats can be distinguished by their fatty acid profile. Some polyunsaturated fatty acids, such as linoleic acid, are essential for life. Animal fats, hard vegetable fats, and coconut fat contain fatty acids that are predominantly saturated. Monounsaturated and polyunsaturated fatty acids help to lower cholesterol levels, and high-quality vegetable oils such as safflower oil, wheat germ oil, sunflower oil, soya oil, and olive oil should be used for preference.

However, fat should not be condemned altogether. It keeps our bodies elastic, stores energy ready for emer-

Bread and cereals with milk (wholemeal bread with yogurt, porridge, granola with sour set milk, rice pudding, and semolina pudding).

Potatoes with eggs, milk, quark, or cheese (fried potatoes with fried egg, mashed potato or baked potatoes with quark).

Legumes with cereals, bread, or eggs (red lentils with rice, lentil soup with bread).

Fat makes you fit - and overweight

Fat can be either of animal or vegetable origin. Both kinds contain exactly the same number of calories - twice the number in carbohydrates and protein. For this reason it is important not to eat too much fat. Fat

overweight, so for this reason you should never eat more than 70 grams (2 1/2 ounces) of fat per day.

Vitamins and minerals

A distinction can be made between water-soluble and fat-soluble vitamins. The water-soluble group includes the eight vitamins of the B-complex and vitamin C. These vitamins are contained in cereals, potatoes, fruit and vegetables, salad, herbs, milk, and cheese. These foods should not be immersed in water for too long.

The fat-soluble vitamins include vitamin A, beta-carotene (a primitive version of vitamin A), and vitamins D, E, and K. It is advisable to eat foods containing fat-soluble vitamins with a little fat. Vitamin A is found exclusively in foodstuffs of animal origin. Beta-carotene is found in all fruit and vegetables that are green or orange in color, vitamin E in vegetable fats and oils, cereals, nuts, and vegetables. Vitamin D is found in fish liver oils, but also in animal and vegetable foodstuffs with high levels of fat, such as avocados, nuts, and eggs. Vitamin K is found in milk products with a high fat content, cereals, cabbage, and spinach.

Minerals are inorganic elements which humans have to ingest via food. They are absolutely essential for blood, bones, nerves, hormones, muscles, and many other vital bodily functions. Since many people suffer from iodine deficiency, iodized table salt is recommended.

It is possible to survive for quite a while without an adequate supply of vitamins and minerals. But at some stage infectious diseases start to take hold, concentration starts to fail, hair falls out and becomes dull, and symptoms such as inflammation of the gums, cracks at the corners of the mouth, broken fingernails, and

gencies (times when food is in short supply, or we are ill), and ensures that our bodies can absorb the fat-soluble vitamins A, D, E, and K. In addition, fat is an excellent vehicle for flavor. Around 30 percent of our energy requirements should be met by fat, an amount that is equivalent to 5 teaspoons of butter, 2 table-spoons of quality vegetable oil, 250 milliliters (1 cup) milk or yogurt, and 100 grams (approximately 3 1/2 ounces) of low-fat cheese. These contain around 65 grams (2 1/4 ounces) of fat, which is the recommended daily intake. People who eat too much fat become eczema may appear. Long-term vitamin deficiency may result in life-threatening diseases.

Vitamins protect against free radicals

Free radicals are aggressive oxygen compounds, which are formed in the body and can be damaging to it. They turn the unsaturated fatty acids present in our bodies into harmful oxidizing agents, resulting in the destruction of the cell wall and ultimately of the cell itself. For this reason, food is extremely important as a supplier of natural antioxidants, which are the substances that protect against oxidizing radicals. The vitamins beta-carotene, C, and E can protect our cells against free radicals. Foodstuffs with antioxidant properties include

bell peppers, citrus fruits, potatoes, berries, nuts and seeds, high-quality vegetable oils, avocados, carrots, apricots, spinach, broccoli, green cabbage, tomatoes, mangos, and papayas.

Water - the elixir of life

It is possible to live for a long time without solid food, but without water death occurs after two or three days. Water serves as a building block for other compounds, as a solvent; as a temperature regulator, and in addition, in the form of blood, it transports a variety of substances around the body. It is a mistake to wait until you are thirsty before reaching for a drink. Under normal circumstances, humans require between 1 1/2 and 2 liters of water a day (approximately 3 to 4 pints/1 1/2 to 2 quarts). In hot temperatures, or when engaged in strenuous work or sport, the fluid intake must be increased. Ordinary tap water, mineral water, herbal tea, and fruit spritzers are recommended, while sodas, alcohol, coffee, and glucose drinks are best avoided. Milk should be regarded as a food rather than as a thirst-quencher.

Vegetables and potatoes

Fresh vegetables are available all year round. In the winter months there is an abundant supply of vitamin-rich varieties of cabbage. Try beets, black salsify, and rutabaga as well. Sauerkraut tastes best in autumn and winter. If you can, try to buy only fresh sauerkraut straight from the vat. If, after cooking, you stir in a handful of fresh sauerkraut, the spicy flavor is enhanced and the vitamin content is increased. In spring, the first radishes, tender carrots and peas, young kohlrabi, tasty spinach, and fine asparagus arrive in the market. While winter vegetables are frequently used for robust stews, young vegetables should be cooked for as short a time as possible and should be served accompanied by a light sauce. In summer, connoisseurs enjoy the first new potatoes, and a wider range of vegetables becomes available - onions, cauliflower, broccoli, zucchini, artichokes, mushrooms, cucumbers, green beans, broad beans, okra, celery, Swiss chard, and fennel make it easy to ring the changes in summer cookery. In autumn the table is laden; the numerous summer vegetables that are still available are supplemented by pumpkin, tomatoes, peppers, corn, potatoes, sweet potatoes, cabbage, leeks, Jerusalem artichokes, turnip-rooted parsley, and celeriac.

Potatoes should be served every day. Whatever you do, try not to buy the same variety all the time. Large and small thin and knobby locally grown varieties are available in markets everywhere. Learn to distinguish the different types by their flavor. Waxy varieties that stay firm when cooked are suitable for fried potatoes, for potatoes boiled in their skins, and for potato salad. The varieties that turn floury when cooked are best for baked potatoes, potato casseroles, and French fries. These varieties should also be used for boiled potatoes, mashed potatoes, fried potato cakes, and potato soups.

Salads, herbs, and shoots

Lettuce and piquant herbs feature strongly in young, fresh cuisine. We can now buy the most delicious lettuce all year round. Iceberg lettuce, once so popular, has now given way to other varieties such as lollo rosso and lollo bianco, oakleaf lettuce, Batavia, frisée, endive, and Romaine lettuce. In autumn and winter, lamb's lettuce, chicory, and radicchio are popular sources of vitamins. Recently, arugula (rocket) has become extremely fashionable. Dandelion is not popular with everyone because of its bitter flavor, and tastes best in mixed salads.

Salad vegetables include tomato, cucumber, fennel, bell peppers, radishes, and onions, which are delicious both raw and as a cooked vegetable. In addition, carrots, celeriac, celery, kohlrabi, white cabbage, leeks, asparagus, and spinach are suitable for plates of crudités.

Chives, parsley, and dill are the most popular herbs. Many culinary herbs can also be bought in small flowerpots. If you look around, you will discover green and red basil, sage, tarragon, lavender, lovage, chervil, coriander, peppermint, thyme, rosemary, marjoram, oregano, lemon thyme, lemon balm, and lemon grass. There is a herb with grayish green leaves that smells strongly of curry and an aromatic plant that smells of pineapple. The flowers of herbs are also edible. Seed companies sell all the popular culinary herbs, and a seed mixture of herbs with edible flowers is available. Delicate fresh herbs are never cooked with other ingredients, with the exception of rosemary, thyme, and bay. Herbs are also available in stores in dried and freeze-dried form. They are used more sparingly than fresh herbs, because their flavor is more intense.

Fresh and dried herbs serve as a decorative garnish for almost any dish (with the exception of sweet dishes), but they have other functions; they often serve as a substitute for salt, they bring out the full flavor of vegetables and sauces, and they can be the source of many a culinary surprise.

Sprouts can easily be grown at home. You will find both the equipment you need and the seeds in organic and health-food stores. Soya bean sprouts, alfalfa sprouts, and mixed sprouts are also available from greengrocers. Try growing radish, mustard, sunflower, and pumpkin seed sprouts. As well as sunflower and pumpkin seeds, legumes are also suitable for growing sprouts. Alfalfa and legume sprouts should be cooked for a few minutes to make them more digestible. Homegrown sprouts are a pure, unadulterated foodstuff. Just try them for yourself - all you need to do is to water the seeds twice daily with fresh water, and in three or four days you will be able to enjoy delicious shoots, packed full of vitamins.

Fruit and berries

Apart from raspberries, all fruits that do not require peeling should be washed under running water and dried on kitchen towel. Smaller fruits such as berries should be thoroughly drained. People with sensitive digestions should peel fruits such as apples and pears.

Fruits and berries taste best fresh and raw, but can also be cooked in a little fruit juice, water, or wine. Buy fruit when there is a glut on the market, in other words at harvest time. In December, strawberries, apricots, and cherries are well out of season, expensive, and often lacking in flavor. Exotic fruits are a welcome alternative in the fruit bowl. Pineapples, bananas, kiwi fruit, star fruit, mangos, papayas, lychees, melons, and citrus fruits contain many vital nutrients. All fruits are rich in secondary nutrients that have a beneficial effect on the human organism. Fresh products are preferable to vitamin pills for this reason.

Cereals and legumes

Cereals contain all the substances that the human body needs, apart from vitamin C. Cereals provide carbohydrates, fiber, protein, fat, vitamins, and minerals. Technological advances have made it possible to mill grain so finely that it is white - and lacking in nutrients. For this reason you should only eat whole grains, and bread and bakery products made with wholemeal flour. Flour graded as type 450 contains hardly any nutrients; the higher the grade, the higher the nutrient value of the flour. Wholemeal flour contains all the nutrients in the endosperm, the husk, and the germ. Wonderful dishes can be prepared using whole, cracked, and milled cereal grains. Look around in your organic or health-food store. As well as wheat, barley, rye, and oats, you will also find spelt, spelt wheat (dried spelt), buckwheat, kamut (an old wheat variety), millet, and quinoa. You may be able to have the cereals cracked or milled while you wait. The flour produced must be used immediately, as it can turn rancid due to the fat content in the germ.

Legumes are universally available, cheap, and rich in carbohydrates, fiber, protein, vitamins, and minerals. There is a wide selection of beans - large and small white beans, pinto beans, various red beans, black beans, light green flageolet beans, soya beans, and mung beans. Familiar lentils include tender red lentils, large split lentils, brown, black, and green lentils, as well as delicate Champagne lentils. Dried peas are a popular choice for winter stews, and are available in stores shelled as well as unshelled. If you have ever tasted round, nutty-flavored chickpeas you will be keen to use them again. Beans, unshelled peas, and chickpeas are best soaked overnight and cooked the next day in fresh salted water. Lentils do not need to be soaked, but soaking for a few hours does reduce the cooking time.

Milk, cheese, and eggs

Milk makes you alert, milk makes you beautiful, and milk is very healthy! With the calcium and high level of protein it contains, milk is not just an indispensable food - it also forms the basis of delicious products such as yogurt, sour milk, kefir, buttermilk, cream, butter, and around 1000 kinds of cheese. Raw milk can only be kept for one or two days, fresh whole milk for about a week. A type of fresh milk is now available that will keep in the refrigerator for around 14 days. Ultrapasteurized (UHT) milk can be kept unrefrigerated for up to three months. The recommended minimum daily allowance of milk is 1/4 liter (1 cup). People who find whole milk indigestible can switch to soured milk products.

Cheese is more than just a delicious accompaniment to bread. Everyone has his own favorite among the many types available. Cheese is best kept in the vegetable compartment of the refrigerator, and removed and left to stand at room temperature for 30 minutes before serving. Cheese used to make a gratin topping should have a minimum fat content of 45% of the dry mass. This means that the dry product contains 45% fat. Hard cheese, such as Emmental with a fat content of 45% of dry mass contains more fat than 100g of a moist Camembert with a fat content of 45% of dry mass. Cheese can be used for gratin toppings, thick slices of cheese can be coated in breadcrumbs and fried, while grated cheese is an indispensable accompaniment to pasta. Cheese is an added refinement in fillings, soups, and stews, adds the finishing touch to every pizza and quiche, and tastes delicious on bread and with wine.

Eggs are a miniature power pack inside a fragile shell. They should always be as fresh as possible and preferably come from free-range hens. Eggs are always kept in the refrigerator. They can be used in such a variety of ways that it would be possible to fill a whole book with egg recipes. Just think of delicious treats such as omelet with fresh mushrooms, scrambled eggs with herbs, pancakes, Huevos Rancheros, egg salad, stuffed eggs, and eggs pickled in brine. Or think of the irresistible desserts, cakes, and tarts that would really taste rather dreadful without eggs. Eggs are graded by weight; S designates the smallest egg, M a medium-sized egg, L a large and XL an extra large egg.

Spices

Entire nations once went to war over pepper, allspice, and cinnamon. Today, we can buy almost any exotic spice for a few dollars. In many kitchens the most frequently used spices are salt, pepper, paprika, caraway, nutmeg, curry powder, and cinnamon. Food can be seasoned perfectly well using these. But try adding a piece of star anise or a tiny piece of cinnamon bark to the water used for boiling carrots, or add sophistication to soups and stews with allspice berries, juniper berries, and coriander seeds, and be extravagant with bay leaves. Add a pinch of saffron to a vanilla pudding to give it a wonderfully appetizing yellow color.

Whole spices keep their unique flavor for longer than the powdered form. Peppercorns, coriander and cardamom seeds, aniseed and fennel, mustard seeds, cloves, cumin, and hot chili peppers are ground or crushed in a mortar and pestle, but can also be cooked whole with the other ingredients. The flavor of these spices is intensified if they are briefly roasted in a pan beforehand. If you want to give your dishes a very special character, grind some bay leaves, various types of peppercorn, star anise, coriander, cardamom, cloves, cinnamon bark, and coarsely chopped nutmeg in a good spice mill. A hint of this mixture, or of a similar blend of spices, will give any dish an exciting new taste.

Fresh spices include ginger, capers, garlic, horseradish, lemon grass, and onions, which, finely chopped or grated, are fundamental to the characteristic flavor of many dishes. If you are not familiar with a spice, use it sparingly at first. If you like the flavor, then add a little more next time. Be adventurous, and make creative use of these precious occidental and oriental spices. But beware: spices should not be allowed to overwhelm the flavor of the dish itself.

Cooking to preserve vitamins

Overcooking destroys many nutrients. Vegetables are best steamed, for as short a time as possible. In kitchen equipment stores today you will find a range of steaming pans of various sizes, or steamers that fit inside your own pans for cooking vegetables over boiling water. Special steamers are now also available for large quantities. If you cook vegetables in salted water, use as little water as possible. If you know your stove and your pans well, it is possible to end up with just a few drops of water in the bottom of the pan at the end of

the cooking time. Vegetables should never be cooked for too long in a covered pan; they taste best al dente.

Stocking up

Buy only as much fruit and vegetables as you will be able to eat within the next few days. With each day that passes, vegetables lose their vitamins. Shriveled apples, bruised and rotten pears, moldy raspberries and strawberries, rubbery carrots and asparagus sticks, and wilted cabbages and herbs have no place on the plate or in the cooking pot. It is better to leave tired-looking fruit and vegetables on the shelf and buy deep-frozen goods instead.

Firm-textured fruits can be stored at room temperature, while berries are best kept in the refrigerator. Delicate fruits such as cherries, grapes, and plums are best eaten on the day of purchase or the day after. Because of their hard outer skin or rind, exotic fruits can be stored for up to a week at room temperature. Firm vegetables such as cabbage, beets, pumpkins, zucchini, eggplants, paprika, and green beans can be kept for several days in the vegetable compartment of the refrigerator, while delicate vegetables such as asparagus and spinach should be prepared on the day of purchase. Leafy salads should also, wherever possible, be eaten the same day. Delicate lettuce leaves can, however, be washed and stored in sealed plastic tubs or plastic bags in the

refrigerator for up to two days. Fresh herbs are washed, chopped, and stored in water, which should be changed every day. Fresh herbs can also be grown on the windowsill, on a balcony, or in the yard.

Potatoes are best stored in a cool cellar or bought weekly from the market. When potatoes stored in the cellar begin to sprout, they should no longer be eaten.

Foods such as sugar, flour, semolina, pasta, rice, custard powder, thickeners for sauces, baking ingredients, nuts, and seeds should be stored separately in sealed containers and inspected from time to time for pests. If a flour moth or maggot has concealed itself in the cupboard, there will be a plentiful supply of food for its offspring. Simple, effective traps for pests that can be fixed to the cupboard door are available from health-food stores.

Let us tempt you with our appetizing suggestions. Try the irresistible recipes featuring vitamin-packed vegetables, potatoes and fruit, milk and cheese, nuts, seeds, and cereals. They are all delicious, and because of the many vital nutrients they contain they will also make you fit and healthy for daily life.

Quantity per 100 g		Energy (kcal)	Protein (g)	Fat (g)	Carbohydrate (g)	Cholesterol (mg)	Magnesium (mg)	Calcium (mg)	Iron (mg)	Vitamin A (µg)	Vitamin E (mg)	Vitamin C (mg)
HERBS	Watercress	18,7	1,6	0,3	2,0	0,0	34,0	180,0	3,1	692,0	1,0	51,0
HERBS	Parsley	52,6	4,4	0,4	7,4	0,0	41,0	245,0	5,5	902,0	3,7	166,0
HERBS	Chives	27,3	3,6	0,6	1,6	0,0	44,0	129,0	1,9	50,0	1,6	47,0
SALAD	Lamb's lettuce	14,4	1,8	0,4	0,7	0,0	13,0	35,0	2,0	650,0	0,6	35,0
SALAD	Head lettuce	11,7	1,3	0,2	1,1	0,0	11,0	37,0	1,0	240,0	0,6	13,0
VEGETABLES	Leaf spinach, cooked	16,0	2,3	0,3	0,4	0,0	36,0	123,0	3,2	723,0	1,4	24,1
VEGETABLES	Celery	16,7	1,2	0,2	2,2	0,0	12,0	80,0	0,5	483,0	0,2	7,0
VEGETABLES	Broccoli	23,2	3,2	0,2	1,9	0,0	23,0	112,0	1,2	137,0	0,7	61,1
VEGETABLES	Fennel	24,6	2,4	0,3	2,8	0,0	49,0	109,0	2,7	783,0	6,0	93,0
VEGETABLES	Asparagus	14,6	1,7	0,1	1,4	0,0	11,0	25,0	0,5	79,0	2,0	9,0
VEGETABLES	Leek	23,0	2,3	0,3	2,5	0,0	12,0	93,0	0,8	168,0	0,6	12,1
VEGETABLES	Aubergine (eggplant)	17,5	1,2	0,2	2,5	0,0	11,0	13,0	0,4	7,0	0,0	2,8
VEGETABLES	Pea	81,8	6,6	0,5	12,3	0,0	33,0	24,0	1,8	72,0	0,3	25,0
VEGETABLES	Beans	25,4	2,4	0,2	3,2	0,0	25,0	63,0	0,8	56,0	0,1	12,2
VEGETABLES	Courgette (zucchini)	19,1	1,6	0,4	2,0	0,0	22,0	30,0	1,5	58,0	0,5	16,0
VEGETABLES	Carrots	25,8	1,0	0,2	4,8	0,0	18,0	41,0	2,1	1574,0	0,5	7,0
VEGETABLES	Cucumber	12,2	0,6	0,2	1,8	0,0	8,0	15,0	0,5	66,0	0,1	8,0
VEGETABLES	Potato	70,3	2,0	0,1	14,6	0,0	19,0	6,0	0,4	1,0	0,1	12,3
VEGETABLES	Tomato	19,6	1,1	0,2	2,9	0,0	15,0	16,0	0,5	94,0	1,0	15,2
VEGETABLES	Paprika	20,3	1,2	0,3	0,3	0,0	12,0	11,0	0,7	180,0	2,8	77,2
VEGETABLES	Onion	28,0	1,3	0,3	4,9	0,0	11,0	31,0	0,5	1,0	0,1	8,1
VEGETABLES	Garlic	141,9	6,1	0,1	28,4	0,0	35,0	38,0	1,4	0,0	0,0	14,0
FRUIT	Apple	51,9	0,3	0,4	11,4	0,0	6,0	7,0	0,5	8,0	0,5	12,0
FRUIT	Pear	52,4	0,5	0,3	12,4	0,0	7,0	9,0	0,3	3,0	0,4	5,0
FRUIT	Apricot	42,3	0,9	0,1	8,5	0,0	10,0	17,0	0,6	298,0	0,5	9,0
FRUIT	Nectarine	56,9	0,9	0,1	12,4	0,0	10,0	4,0	0,5	73,0	0,5	8,0
FRUIT	Peach	40,7	0,8	0,1	8,9	0,0	9,0	7,0	0,5	73,0	1,0	10,0
FRUIT	Strawberry	32,1	0,8	0,4	5,5	0,0	15,0	25,0	1,0	8,0	0,1	65,0
FRUIT	Raspberry	34,0	1,3	0,3	4,8	0,0	30,0	40,0	1,0	3,0	0,9	25,0
FRUIT	Grape	71,1	0,7	0,3	15,6	0,0	9,0	18,0	0,5	4,0	0,7	4,0
FRUIT	Pineapple	58,9	0,5	0,2	13,1	0,0	17,0	16,0	0,4	10,0	0,1	19,0
FRUIT	Banana	95,2	1,1	0,2	21,4	0,0	36,0	9,0	0,6	38,0	0,3	12,0
	Walnut	655,0	14,4	62,5	10,6	0,0	130,0	87,0	2,5	8,0	6,0	2,6

Quantity per 100 g		Energy (kcal)	Protein (g)	Fat (g)	Carbohydrate (g)	Cholesterol (mg)	Magnesium (mg)	Calcium (mg)	Iron (mg)	Vitamin A (µg)	Vitamin E (mg)	Vitamin C (mg)
NUTS	Hazelnut (filbert)	636,8	12,0	61,6	10,5	0,0	155,0	225,0	3,8	5,0	26,3	3,0
	Brazil nut	661,0	13,6	66,8	3,5	0,0	160,0	132,0	3,4	0,0	7,6	0,7
	Almond	570,0	18,7	54,1	3,7	0,0	220,0	250,0	4,1	20,0	26,1	0,8
MILK & CHEESE	Low-fat milk	48,6	3,4	1,6	4,9	6,0	12,0	120,0	0,1	14,0	0,0	1,0
	Kefir	49,8	3,4	1,5	4,1	6,0	12,0	120,0	0,1	22,0	0,0	1,0
	Yoghurt (1%)	38,0	4,3	0,1	4,2	1,0	13,0	140,0	0,1	1,0	0,0	1,0
	Parmesan	440,0	32,3	34,8	0,0	82,0	44,0	1200,0	0,6	415,0	1,0	0,0
	Camembert	288,8	21,0	22,8	0,0	70,0	20,0	500,0	0,3	362,0	0,5	0,0
	Sheep's cheese	236,8	17,0	18,8	0,0	45,0	25,0	450,0	0,6	228,0	0,5	0,0
	Feta	236,8	17,0	18,8	0,0	45,0	25,0	450,0	0,6	228,0	0,5	0,0
	Mozzarella	255,0	19,0	19,8	0,0	46,0	20,0	403,0	0,3	297,0	0,6	0,0
OILS & VEGET. FATS	Olive oil	882,5	0,0	99,6	0,2	1,0	0,0	1,0	0,1	157,0	12,1	0,0
	Vegetable oil	883,5	0,0	99,8	0,0	1,0	1,0	1,0	0,0	4,0	62,5	0,0
	Sesame oil	881,6	0,2	99,5	0,0	1,0	0,0	10,0	0,1	0,0	3,5	0,0
	Soya oil	872,7	0,0	98,6	0,0	2,0	0,0	0,0	0,0	583,0	17,0	0,0
	Sunflower oil	883,5	0,0	99,8	0,0	1,0	1,0	1,0	0,0	4,0	62,5	0,0
	Butter	741,9	0,7	83,2	0,6	240,0	3,0	13,0	0,1	653,0	2,0	0,2
	Egg yolk	349,0	16,1	31,9	0,3	1260,0	16,0	140,0	7,2	886,0	5,7	0,0
	Egg white	49,8	11,1	0,2	0,7	0,0	12,0	11,0	0,2	0,0	0,0	0,3

Breakfast & snacks

Yoghurt with fruit

The first meal of the day should always be varied and very light. Fresh fruit yoghurt is easy and quick to prepare and the fruit can be varied depending on the season and on what is available.

1 Put the yoghurt, maple syrup and oat bran in a deep bowl and stir well. Wash the blackberries and dab dry. Peel the banana, cut into slices and sprinkle with lemon juice. Peel the kiwi fruit and cut it into slices .

2 Garnish the yoghurt with the sliced banana and kiwi fruit. Fry the oat flakes without oil in a non-stick pan until light brown. Leave to cool and sprinkle over the fruit.

Serves 1. About 290 kcal per serving

125 g/4 1/2 oz low-fat yoghurt
  (1.5%)

1 teaspoon maple syrup

1 teaspoon oat bran

50 g/2 oz blackberries

1/2 banana

1 teaspoon lemon juice

1 kiwi fruit

2 tablespoons oat flakes

Nectarine yoghurt

A fruity breakfast which is quick and easy to prepare. Instead of nectarine you can also use half a mango.

1 Wash the nectarine carefully, pat dry, remove the stone (pit) and purée with a hand-mixer in a tall beaker. Stir in the yoghurt and sweeten with maple syrup.

2 Fry the oat flakes in a non-stick frying pan without oil. Leave to cool briefly and stir into the yoghurt mixture. Put the nectarine yoghurt in a muesli bowl and sprinkle with almond flakes.

Serves 1. About 280 kcal per serving

1 ripe nectarine

125 g/4 1/2 oz low-fat yoghurt
  (1.5%)

1 tablespoon maple syrup

2 tablespoons oat flakes

1 teaspoon flaked (slivered)
  almonds

Three-grain muesli with sour milk

The various ingredients for this three-grain muesli are available in health food shops and in some supermarkets with a good health food section. You can also prepare a large amount of muesli in advance and store it in a jar with a screw-top lid where it will keep for up to four weeks.

1 Place the wheat, spelt and barley in a large bowl and stir well. Add honey pops and raisins.

2 Put the sunflower seeds in a non-stick pan and fry briefly without oil. Allow to cool down and add to the cereal mixture.

3 Peel an apple, cut it in half and remove the core. Grate one apple half finely and add to the cereal mixture. Pour the sour milk over the cereal mixture, stir well and leave to stand for a few minutes. Garnish with the hazelnuts (filberts) before serving.

Serves 1. About 360 kcal per serving

1 tablespoon wheat flakes

1 tablespoon spelt flakes

1 tablespoon barley flakes

1 tablespoon honey pops (puffed wheat, coated with honey)

1 teaspoon raisins

1 teaspoon sunflower seeds

1/2 apple

125 g/41/2 oz sour milk

4–5 hazelnuts (filberts)

Cinnamon muesli with raspberries

3 tablespoons oat flakes

2 pinches cinnamon

1 teaspoon maple syrup

1 tablespoon cornflakes

3 tablespoons low-fat quark

2 tablespoons low-fat milk (1.5%)

1 teaspoon flaked (slivered) almonds

1–2 tablespoons raspberries

This delicious muesli is quick and easy to prepare. You can also use bilberries (blueberries) or blackberries instead of raspberries.

❶ Put the oats, cinnamon and maple syrup in a deep bowl and stir well. Add the cornflakes and stir again.

❷ Pour the low-fat quark and milk into a small bowl, stir until smooth and pour over the cereal mixture. Sprinkle with almond flakes.

❸ Wash the raspberries, dab dry and garnish the muesli with them.

Serves 1. About 260 kcal per serving

Fruit muesli

1 tablespoon walnuts

1 tablespoon berries, for instance, strawberries or blackberries

1/2 banana

1/2 pear

1 teaspoon lemon juice

3 tablespoons spelt flakes

1 small carton low-fat yoghurt (1.5%)

1 pinch cinnamon

1 teaspoon honey

Fresh fruit muesli makes a delicious and healthy breakfast. The fruit is full of vitamins and minerals, while the cereals provide all the necessary energy needed by the body to start the day.

❶ Chop the walnuts coarsely. Wash and prepare the berries. Peel the bananas, wash and prepare the pears. Cut the fruit into bite-sized pieces, put it all in a bowl and sprinkle with lemon juice.

❷ Fry the spelt flakes briefly in a non-stick pan without any oil. Leave to cool and pour them over the fruit.

❸ Put the honey and cinnamon in a small bowl and stir well to obtain a smooth mixture. Pour over the fruit and spelt flakes. Finally sprinkle the coarsely chopped walnuts over the muesli, and leave to stand for a few minutes.

Serves 1. About 415 kcal per serving

Fresh cereal muesli with strawberries

A cereal mill is invaluable for preparing your own muesli. It is an excellent idea to grind the cereals yourself because freshly ground cereals retain their vitamins and minerals better. However, ready-ground cereal can be bought in health food shops. The crushed oats used in this muesli are soaked in apple juice overnight.

❶ Put the crushed oats in a large muesli bowl, add the apple juice and leave to soak overnight.

❷ Put the yoghurt, rosehip purée and grated orange zest in a bowl and stir well. Add the crushed oats and stir well again.

❸ Add the raspberries to the yoghurt and crushed oats mixture and stir carefully. Sprinkle the sunflower seeds over the muesli.

Serves 1. About 330 kcal per serving

2 tablespoons crushed oats

100 ml/3 1/2 fl oz (1/2 cup) unsweetened apple juice

100 g/3 1/2 oz low-fat yoghurt (1.5%)

1 tablespoon honey-sweetened rosehip purée

1 pinch grated untreated orange zest

100 g/3 1/2 oz strawberries

1 tablespoon sunflower seeds

Quark with crunchy cereal flakes

Low-fat quark is ideal for breakfast – it contains very little fat and a lot of protein. Ready mixed cereal flakes such as wheat, spelt and barley are available in health food shops.

❶ Put the low-fat quark in a bowl with the vanilla sugar and milk and stir to make a smooth mixture.

❷ Heat the honey in a small non-stick pan, add the mixed cereals and fry until golden brown, stirring continuously. Remove the pan from the heat, leave the honey and cereal mixture to cool down, then pour over the quark. Sprinkle grated coconut on top.

Serves 1. About 330 kcal per serving

150 g/5 oz low-fat quark

1 teaspoon vanilla sugar

2 tablespoons low-fat milk (1.5%)

1 tablespoon wild honey

2 tablespoons mixed cereal flakes

1 tablespoon grated coconut

Bread with fresh strawberries

2 slices wholemeal (whole grain) rye bread

2 teaspoons low-fat fromage frais

150 g/5 oz strawberries

1 teaspoon lemon juice

freshly ground black pepper

2 mint leaves

A delicious, light breakfast for everyone who loves strawberries: wholemeal (wholewheat) bread with fromage frais topped with a thick layer of sliced strawberries which can be seasoned with a little pepper.

❶ Spread fromage frais on the slices of rye bread. Wash the strawberries, dab dry and remove the stalks. Cut the strawberries into slices and sprinkle with lemon juice.

❷ Arrange the sliced strawberries on the bread. Season with freshly ground pepper. Wash the mint leaves, dab dry, chop finely and sprinkle over the strawberries.

Serves 1. About 175 kcal per serving

Pear quark with crispbread

Quark is very versatile. It can be combined in all sorts of ways with fruit and cereals and has the advantage of containing very little fat. The yeast flakes can be bought in health food shops; they contain large amounts of B-vitamins which play a vital part in the formation of blood.

200 g/7 oz low-fat quark

2 tablespoons low-fat milk (1.5%)

1 pear

1 teaspoon honey

1 tablespoon spelt flakes

1 teaspoon yeast flakes

2 slices crispbread

❶ Put the low-fat quark and milk in a bowl and stir to make a smooth mixture. Wash the pear, cut into quarters and remove the core. Cut into very small cubes and stir into the quark.

❷ Sweeten the quark with honey and add the spelt flakes. Leave to stand for a few minutes.

❸ Put the pear yoghurt into a small bowl and sprinkle the yeast flakes on top. Serve with crispbread.

Serves 1. About 410 kcal per serving

Crispbread with banana and bread with tomato

A sweet and savoury open sandwich, rich in nutrients and with very little fat. Instead of the banana, you could use peach slices.

❶ Spread 1 tablespoon cottage cheese on a slice of crispbread. Peel the banana, cut into slices and arrange on the crispbread with cottage cheese. Slice the hazelnuts (filberts) and place on the banana slices. Add the honey if desired.

❷ Spread the remaining cottage cheese on the slice of wholemeal bread. Wash the tomato, remove the stalk, cut into eight pieces and arrange on the bread. Wash the parsley, chop the leaves finely and sprinkle over the tomatoes. Season with a little salt and freshly ground pepper.

❸ Arrange the crispbread topped with banana and the wholemeal (wholewheat) bread with tomatoes on a large platter.

Serves 1. About 310 kcal per serving

1 slice crispbread

2 tablespoons cottage cheese

1/2 small banana

2–3 shelled hazelnuts (filberts)

a little honey (optional)

1 slice wholemeal (wholewheat) bread

1 tomato

3 sprigs parsley

salt

freshly ground pepper

Unleavened bread with tomatoes and yoghurt

An interesting vegetarian dish which should be served on a plate and eaten with a knife and fork; this is the best way to enjoy the refreshing yoghurt sauce which combines so well with the bread.

❶ Cut the tomatoes into small cubes and slice the peeled onions wafer-thin. Coarsely chop the parsley.

❷ Put the yoghurt in a bowl and stir vigorously with a whisk until smooth. Mix together the diced tomatoes, onion rings, parsley, sugar and seasoning. Add lemon juice to taste.

❸ Cut the unleavened bread into 8 slices and cut in half horizontally. Place the bread slices on four plates and cover with the tomato and yoghurt mixture.

Serves 4. About 131 kcal per serving

800 g/1 3⁄4 lb ripe sweet tomatoes

2 red onions

1 bunch smooth parsley

500 ml/17 fl oz (2 1/4 cups) yoghurt

sugar

salt

cayenne pepper

paprika

1 tablespoon lemon juice

1 loaf unleavened (matzo) bread

butter for the baking dish

8 large ripe tomatoes

4 tablespoons breadcrumbs

2 teaspoons salt

2 teaspoons white pepper

1 teaspoon tarragon

4 tablespoons honey

40 g/1 1/2 oz (3 tablespoons) butter

Baked honey tomatoes

A sweet temptation. The honey brings out the tomato's own sweet flavour while the tarragon, salt and pepper add a spicy note to the dish.

❶ Pre-heat the oven to 200°C (400°F), Gas mark 6. Generously butter a large oven-proof dish.

❷ Cut the top off each tomato at the end opposite the stalk to open up the seed vessels; reserve the "lids". Put the tomatoes on some kitchen paper with the cut end downward so that the seeds and juices run out. Carefully remove the remaining seeds with the tip of a knife. Put the tomatoes stalk end downwards in the oven-proof dish.

❸ Add salt, pepper and tarragon to the breadcrumbs and mix well. Put the honey in the tomatoes and add the breadcrumb mixture on top. Put a teaspoon of butter on each tomato and put the lid back on.

❹ Bake the honey tomatoes in the oven for about 20 minutes. Then put under the oven grill at maximum temperature for about 5 minutes. Serve hot.

Serves 4. About 210 kcal per serving

Bread with cheese topping and apple garnish

As is well-known, one should eat an apple a day because they contain a lot of important vitamins and minerals. As a result, this breakfast is undoubtedly one of the healthiest ways of starting the day!

❶ Put the cottage cheese, maple syrup, grated coconut and cinnamon in a bowl and stir well.

❷ Wash the apple, cut into quarters and remove the core. Cut the apple quarters into thin slices and sprinkle with lemon juice.

❸ Spread the cottage cheese mixture on the slice of wholemeal bread and garnish with the apple slices.

Serves 1. About 340 kcal per serving

100 g/3 1⁄2 oz cottage cheese
1 tablespoon maple syrup
1 tablespoon grated coconut
1 pinch cinnamon
1 apple
1 teaspoon cinnamon
1 slice wholemeal (wholewheat)
   bread

Fromage frais and apple open sandwich

A tasty sandwich for people who prefer a savoury breakfast: wholemeal bread with fromage frais will satisfy your hunger and set you up for the whole day.

❶ Spread the fromage frais on the slice of wholemeal bread and sprinkle a little paprika on top.

❷ Wash the cress and dab dry. Sprinkle the cress and sunflower seeds over the fromage frais.

❸ Wash the apple, cut into eight pieces and remove the core. Garnish the bread and fromage frais with the pieces of apple and arrange on a flat platter.

Serves 1. About 360 kcal per serving

1 slice wholemeal (wholewheat)
   bread
20 g/3⁄4 oz low-fat fromage frais
paprika
1 tablespoon cress
1 tablespoon sunflower seeds
1 apple

Wholemeal bread with herb quark

An ideal breakfast with plenty of fibre and protein which will satisfy your hunger while being very low in calories. This open sandwich also makes an ideal snack.

❶ Put the low-fat quark and milk in a bowl and stir until smooth. Season with sea salt, paprika and freshly ground pepper.

❷ Peel the onion and chop very finely. Wash the chives and chop finely. Wash the cress and dab dry. Chop half the cress finely and stir into the quark with the onion and herbs.

❸ Spread the herb quark on the slice of wholemeal bread and garnish with the rest of the cress.

Serves 1. About 260 kcal per serving

70 g/3 oz low-fat quark

1 tablespoon milk

freshly ground pepper

1 pinch paprika

sea salt

1 small onion

1/2 bunch chives

2 tablespoons cress

2 slices wholemeal (wholewheat) bread

1 slice pumpkin seed bread

1 tablespoon low-fat quark

1 teaspoon marmalade or fruit spread as preferred

1 clementine or 1 small orange

Pumpkin seed bread with orange marmalade

Lovers of bread and marmalade need not give it up in a low-fat diet, but the marmalade should have a high fruit content and contain as little sugar as possible. The sugar should be cane sugar, and such marmalade can be found in most health food shops.

❶ Spread the low-fat quark on the pumpkin seed bread and cover with the orange marmalade or other reduced-sugar fruit preserve.

❷ Peel the clementine or orange and cut into eight pieces. Arrange them with the bread on a plate.

Serves 1. About 160 kcal per serving

Scrambled egg with celery on bread

1 egg

salt

freshly ground pepper

1/2 bunch chives

1 teaspoon sunflower oil

1 slice wholemeal (wholewheat)
spelt bread

1 teaspoon diet margarine

1/2 stick (stalk) celery with leaves

An ideal breakfast for the weekend when you have enough time to treat yourself to scrambled eggs. Because eggs are very high in cholesterol, one should not indulge in this kind of breakfast more than once or twice a week.

❶ Beat the egg in a bowl using a whisk and season with a little salt and pepper. Wash the chives, chop finely and add to the beaten egg.

❷ Heat the oil in a small non-stick pan, add the egg and allow to thicken for a few minutes over a low flame, stirring with a fork.

❸ Spread diet margarine on a slice of wholemeal (wholewheat) spelt bread. Remove the celery leaves, wash and put to one side. Wash the celery stick (stalk), cut into very thin slices and arrange on the bread. Serve on a plate with the scrambled egg and garnish with the celery leaves.

Serves 1. About 315 kcal per serving

Bruschetta

The supreme light Italian snack: slices of white bread, toasted, topped with diced tomatoes and seasoned with herbs. Served before the starter (appetizer), it sharpens the appetite. It is also a delicious accompaniment to an Italian country wine, such as Montepulciano d'Abruzzo.

4 medium tomatoes

1/2 bunch basil

1/2 bunch parsley

1 clove garlic

salt

pepper

8 slices white bread

4 tablespoons olive oil

❶ Cut the tomatoes into quarters and remove the seeds. Dice the tomato quarters. Coarsely chop the basil and parsley. Peel and chop the cloves of garlic.

❷ Mix the herbs and diced tomatoes in a bowl, add the chopped garlic and season with salt and pepper.

❸ Toast some slices of white bread and sprinkle with olive oil. Put some of the tomato mixture on each slice of toast. Serve immediately.

Serves 4. About 294 kcal per serving

Parmesan and tomato muffins

Quick and easy to prepare, this is a party hit which looks very decorative on a cold buffet table. The Parmesan may be replaced by freshly grated Pecorino, an Italian hard cheese made from sheep's milk.

❶ Pre-heat the oven to 180°C (350°F), Gas mark 4. Mix the flour, cornflour (starch), baking powder, salt and Parmesan in a bowl. Stir in the egg, oil and milk.

❷ Grease the hollows of a muffin tin with oil and fill with the dough. Bake for about 20 minutes in the pre-heated oven. Remove the muffins from the mould and leave to cool on a cake rack.

❸ Cut the cherry tomatoes into slices. Cut the muffins in half horizontally. Cover with the sliced tomato and rocket and serve at once.

Serves 4. About 550 kcal per serving

130 g/5 oz (1 1/4 cups) flour

75 g/3 oz (9 tablespoons) maize flour

2 teaspoons baking powder

1/2 teaspoon salt

150 g/5 oz (1 1/2 cups) freshly grated Parmesan

1 egg, room temperature

60 ml/3 fl oz (6 tablespoons) oil

250 ml/8 fl oz (1 cup) milk

oil for the moulds

8–10 cherry tomatoes

50 g/2 oz rocket

Green tomatoes with cucumbers

This recipe is ideal for anyone who stands in their vegetable garden in the autumn and wonders what to do with all the green tomatoes which refuse to turn red.

❶ Pre-heat the oven at its lowest setting, 80°C (175°F). Cover a baking sheet with kitchen paper.

❷ Cut the tomatoes and peeled cucumber into slices 1 cm/3⁄8 in thick.

❸ Heat equal amounts of butter and oil in a large frying pan

❹ Dip the tomato and cucumber slices in condensed milk and coat on both sides with rolled oats. Carefully fry a few at a time on both sides until the vegetables begin to turn brown.

❺ Place the fried tomatoes and cucumbers on the baking sheet and put in the oven to keep warm. Season with salt and pepper before serving

Serves 4. About 225 kcal per serving

6 large green tomatoes (already showing some traces of orange)

1 cucumber

butter and oil for frying

1–2 cups condensed milk

1–2 cups fine porridge (rolled) oats

salt

pepper

Ciabatta with leaf spinach and tomato filling

Ciabatta is a particularly crusty type of Italian white bread. This delicious leaf spinach and tomato filling is also very good on a baguette.

1 Peel the shallots, cut into small cubes and sweat in some oil until transparent. Peel the garlic, press it and add to the shallots. Add the frozen spinach and cook gently for about 15 minutes. Season with salt, pepper and nutmeg.

2 Pre-heat the oven to 200°C (400°F), Gas mark 6.

3 Cut the tomatoes and Camembert into slices. Cut the ciabatta in half and cut each half open. Spread a thin layer of herb butter on the bottom half of each piece of ciabatta and arrange the tomato slices on top. Spoon the spinach mixture on top and cover with slices of camembert.

4 Place the pieces of ciabatta covered with tomato, spinach and camembert on a baking sheet and put in the oven to brown for a maximum of 10 minutes. After about 5 minutes, put the halves without topping in the oven as well.

5 Take the ciabatta with leaf-spinach and tomato topping and serve hot. The other halves can either be put next to each piece or on top.

Serves 4. About 491 kcal per serving

2 shallots

1 tablespoon oil

1 clove garlic

450 g/1 lb leaf spinach, frozen

salt

white pepper

nutmeg

250 g/9 oz soft Camembert

600 g/1 1/4 lb tomatoes

2 ciabatta (about 250 g/9 oz each)

50 g/2 oz (4 tablespoons) herb butter

55 g/2 oz (1/4 cup) sugar
750 g/1 3/4 lb tomatoes
100 ml/3 1/2 fl oz (1/2 cup) gin
juice of 1 lime
sliced lime for the garnish

Tomato sorbet with gin

A sorbet is a semi-frozen dessert made from fruit pulp which was invented by the ancient Persians. It is often served with alcohol as a refreshment just before the main course of a large meal.

1 Bring the sugar to the boil with 100 ml/3 1/2 fl oz (scant 1/2 cup) water. Simmer gently until the sugar has completely dissolved, stirring constantly. Remove from the heat and leave to cool.

2 Peel the tomatoes, cut into quarters and remove the seeds. Chop the tomato pieces finely and put in a saucepan. Simmer over a low heat for about 20 minutes, stirring occasionally.

3 Purée the tomatoes with the sugar solution in a liquidizer or with a hand-mixer. Put this mixture in a freezer box and put in the freezer compartment. Stir from time to time with a whisk as it freezes.

4 Divide the tomato sorbet into six portions and put them in cold glasses or glass bowls. Mix the gin and lime juice and sprinkle over the sorbet. Garnish with slices of lime and serve immediately.

Serves 6. About 86 kcal per serving

Fried cheese cubes

"Manchego", a sheep's milk cheese from the La Mancha region with a strong taste, is used for this tapas dish. Other hard or semi-hard cheeses may be used alternatively. The hot cheese cubes are served as appetizers together with white grapes and an aperitif.

❶ Remove cheese rind and dice cheese into 2 cm cubes.

❷ Beat eggs with cream and pour into a bowl. Mix cornmeal with finely ground almonds and pour into a small bowl. Put flour into a shallow dish.

❸ Roll cheese cubes in flour first, then coat with beaten eggs and finally with the mixture of cornmeal and almonds.

❹ Heat olive oil in a large pan and fry serving portions of cheese cubes until golden brown. Drain on kitchen paper and serve hot.

Serves 4. About 350 kcal per serving

400 g Spanish Manchego, medium hard to hard

2 eggs

1 teaspoon cream

cornmeal

50 g almonds, finely ground

flour

250 ml olive oil

Breaded mangel sticks

Spain boasts of a large variety of breaded, fried and deep-fat fried vegetable dishes. Here is a recipe with mangel sticks.

❶ Blanch mangel sticks and dry well.

❷ Coat in flour, then in beaten eggs and finally in breading.

❸ Heat olive oil (2 fingers high) in a cast-iron pan and fry breaded mangel sticks to a golden brown. Season with salt and serve.

Serves 4. About 440 kcal per serving

12-15 mangel sticks

flour

4 eggs

200 g cornmeal

olive oil

salt

Grilled peppers

A plain tapa dish that tastes lovely with Rioja wine and goes well as an appetizer together with pickled olives and salted almonds.

100 g mild green peppers

100 g mild red peppers

coarse sea salt

a few basil leaves

❶ Preheat oven to 200 °C (400° F). Rinse green and red peppers and put on grill.

❷ Roast peppers for about 20 minutes in oven, take them out and sprinkle with coarse sea salt.

❸ Garnish grilled peppers with basil leaves and serve while still hot.

Serves 4. About 20 kcal per serving

Marinated cauliflower

A savoury vegetable tapas easy to prepare that acquires its delicious flavour only after a few hours of marinating: the cauliflower flowerets are steamed and then left to soak in a marinade of vinegar and oil.

1 small cauliflower

salt

1 tablespoon lemon juice

2 cloves of garlic

2 spring onions

1 stick celery

3 tablespoons olive oil

4 tablespoons white wine
    vinegar

salt

freshly ground white pepper

1 bunch chives

❶ Wash cauliflower, break into flowerets and cook in a pot with salted water and lemon juice for about 5-8 minutes. Test to sample: the cauliflower should be just tender and should not fall apart. Drain cauliflower. Do not discard cooking water.

❷ Peel garlic cloves and slice finely. Clean spring onions and celery sticks, wash and cut into thin pieces, sauté in olive oil.

❸ Pour 4 tablespoons of cooking water and 4 tablepspoons of white wine vinegar over vegetable, bring to a boil briefly and leave to simmer over low heat for about 3 minutes.

❹ Season vegetable stock and vegetables with salt and pepper and pour over flowerets. Wash chives, cut into thin rolls and sprinkle over cauliflower. Leave tapas to cool for at least 2 hours.

Serves 4. About 170 kcal per serving

Sautéed mushrooms

Fresh field mushrooms are available throughout the year. Seasoned with fresh herbs such as parsley or aromatic thyme, you have a delicious tapas dish which is easy to prepare as well. Other mushrooms such as the agaric which is very common in Spain may be substituted.

❶ Clean mushrooms from any remaining soil and cut out spots and bruised parts. Quarter and sprinkle with lemon juice.

❷ Heat olive oil in a pan.

❸ Clean spring onions, wash and cut into thin pieces. You may use part of the green stalk as well, as long as it is tender. Peel garlic cloves, chop coarsely and sauté in pan with spring onions for about 2 minutes.

❹ Stir in mushroom quarters and lemon juice, cover and leave to simmer for a few minutes. Check for doneness – the mushrooms should be just tender.

❺ Season mushrooms with salt and pepper, wash herbs, mince leaves and sprinkle over mushrooms. Serve with toasted white bread.

Serves 4. About 160-200 kcal per serving

500 g small field mushrooms

3 tablespoons lemon juice

3 tablespoons olive oil

3 spring onions

3 cloves garlic

salt

pepper

1/2 bunch parsley or a few thyme sprigs

Salads

Broccoli and asparagus salad

500 g/18 oz green asparagus

250 g/9 oz broccoli

sea salt

1 tablespoon lemon juice

1 pinch sugar

freshly ground pepper

1 tablespoon white wine vinegar

1 teaspoon olive oil

1 tablespoon sesame seeds

This green salad is a real "energy pack" because green vegetables like broccoli are particularly rich in vitamins and minerals. Asparagus also has cleansing properties when prepared as here with a little oil. The cooking liquid can also be used for other dishes: for instance, it makes a delicious stock (broth) for vegetable soup.

❶ Wash the green asparagus. Remove the woody end and peel. Cut into pieces 5 cm/2 in long. Wash the broccoli and divide into small florets.

❷ Heat about 500 ml/17 fl oz (2 1⁄4 cups) water seasoned with a little salt in a large saucepan. Add the asparagus and broccoli. Cover and simmer over a low flame for about 10 minutes. Remove the vegetables from the saucepan and drain. Reserve the cooking liquid.

❸ Put the lemon juice, sugar, salt, pepper and white wine vinegar in a bowl, add 4 tablespoons of the cooking liquid and the olive oil and stir until you obtain a smooth dressing. Pour the dressing over vegetables while they are hot and leave to stand for 30 minutes.

❹ Fry the sesame seed in a non-stick pan without oil and sprinkle over the salad.

Serves 2. About 131 kcal per serving

Potato salad with herb-yoghurt sauce

This potato salad owes its spicy, aromatic flavour to the addition of a light yoghurt dressing with plenty of fresh herbs. It is delicious when freshly prepared and served still slightly warm as a little snack, but it also makes a very tasty accompaniment to braised chicken breast.

❶ Put the potatoes in a steamer. Fill the bottom with water and cook the potatoes for about 20–25 minutes until tender. Peel the potatoes and cut into quarters.

❷ Peel the apple, cut into eight pieces and remove the core. Sprinkle lemon juice on the apple pieces. Wash, top and tail the courgette (zucchini) and slice finely. Peel the onions and chop finely. Wash the radishes, top and tail and slice. Arrange the potatoes, sliced fruit and vegetables on two plates.

❸ Stir the yoghurt and salad cream together and season with vinegar, salt and pepper. Wash the chives and chop finely. Wash the cress and rocket, dab dry and chop coarsely. Add the herbs to the yoghurt and salad cream mixture and pour over the vegetables.

Serves 2. About 205 kcal per serving

400 g/14 oz small waxy potatoes
1 apple
1 teaspoon lemon juice
1 small courgette (zucchini)
1 small onion
1/2 bunch radishes
70 g/3 oz low-fat yoghurt (1.5%)
1 tablespoon low-fat mayonnaise
1 tablespoon white wine vinegar
sea salt
freshly ground pepper
1 bunch chives
2 tablespoons cress
50 g/2 oz rocket

Asparagus salad with new potatoes

Asparagus and new potatoes, the ingredients of this particular salad, complement each most beautifully.

1 kg/2 1/4 lb potatoes

500 g/18 oz green asparagus

salt

1 onion

1 soft-boiled (soft-cooked) egg

2 tablespoons vinegar

2 tablespoons olive oil

freshly ground pepper

1 bunch parsley

❶ Wash the potatoes and boil in their skins. Wash the asparagus and remove the woody ends. Cut the asparagus in to pieces 2 cm/3⁄4 in long and cook in 250 ml/8 fl oz (1 cup) salted boiling water for about 10 minutes until done. Remove from the water and drain.

❷ Bring the asparagus water back to the boil. Pour 2 or 3 tablespoons of it over the peeled, finely chopped onion in the salad bowl, discarding the rest. Shell the hard-boiled egg, dice it and add to the onion mixture. Mix the vinegar, oil, salt and pepper to make a marinade. Pour into the salad bowl and stir well.

❸ Peel the potatoes and cut into slices; add them still hot to the marinade.

❹ Carefully mix together the washed, finely chopped parsley, asparagus and potatoes.

Serves 4. About 243 kcal per serving

Pasta and courgette (zucchini) salad

Courgettes have a slightly nutty taste which is enhanced by the addition of cashew nuts in this salad. Choose small courgettes (zucchini) because they have more taste than the large ones and are therefore better suited for use in salads.

❶ Bring 1 litre/1 3⁄4 pints (4 1⁄2 cups) water to the boil in a saucepan. Add the wholemeal (wholewheat) pasta and season with a pinch of salt. Cook the pasta "al dente" and drain.

❷ Wash and top and tail the courgette. Prepare the mushrooms and wipe them very carefully with kitchen paper. Cut both into fine slices. Make a dressing with lemon juice, white wine, salad cream and pepper.

❸ Put the pasta in a small salad bowl and add the mushrooms and courgettes (zucchini). Pour over the dressing and stir to coat all the ingredients. Coarsely chop the cashew nuts and sprinkle over the pasta salad.

Serves 2. About 330 kcal per serving

salt

50 g/2 oz wholemeal (wholewheat) pasta

1 small courgette (zucchini)

3 large mushrooms

1 tablespoon lemon juice

1 tablespoon white wine

1 tablespoon low-fat salad cream

freshly ground pepper

5 cashew nuts

Tofu salad with asparagus

Tofu (bean curd), soy sauce and ginger are very popular ingredients in Oriental cuisine and their light, spicy aroma complements the delicate taste of the asparagus.

❶ Wash the asparagus, remove the woody ends. Cut off the asparagus tips and keep them separate. Cut the rest into pieces 5 cm/2 in long. Bring water to the boil with 1 tablespoon of soya sauce and cook the asparagus tips for 3 minutes. Remove from the water, drain and put to one side. Add the rest of the pieces to the water and cook for 5 minutes, then drain.

❷ To make the salad dressing: mix 4 tablespoons soy sauce, lemon juice, grated lemon zest, sugar and sunflower oil and stir well.

❸ Cut the tofu into cubes. Wash and trim the spring onion (scallion). Peel the red onion. Cut both into rings. Pull the leaves off the watercress. Mix all the ingredients with the asparagus pieces, stirring very carefully.

❹ Peel the ginger, grate finely and sprinkle over the salad. Garnish with the asparagus tips.

Serves 4. About 215 kcal per serving

450 g/1 lb green asparagus

5 tablespoons soy sauce

juice and zest of 1/2 untreated lemon

3 teaspoons sugar

5 tablespoons sunflower oil

300 g/11 oz tofu (bean curd)

1 spring onion (scallion)

1 red onion

30 g/1 oz watercress

piece of fresh ginger, about 3 cm/1 1/4 in long

Gratiné goat's cheese on a bed of melon

A refreshing, summery snack with a sweet and sour dressing. Served with some crisp white bread, this refined salad is also ideal for a light evening meal.

1 Wash and prepare the mangetout (snow peas). Cut the pods in half. Peel the carrots and cut them into thin slices. Heat up the stock (broth) and cook the vegetables in it for about 5 minutes. Drain them and reserve the cooking liquid.

2 Preheat the oven to 200°C (400°F), Gas mark 6. Remove the seeds from the melon, cut into slices and peel. Put the cheeses in a small ovenproof dish, sprinkle with thyme and pour 1 teaspoon maple syrup on top. Bake the cheeses in the oven for about 10 minutes until they begin to melt.

3 Mix the mustard, remaining maple syrup, cider vinegar, 1 tablespoon stock (broth), herb salt, pepper and capers together to make a dressing and whisk in the walnut oil.

4 Arrange the salad and melon slices on two plates and put the cheeses on top. Pour the dressing over the salad. Sprinkle chopped walnuts on top.

Serves 2. About 295 kcal per serving

80 g/3 oz mangetout (snow peas)

2 young carrots

50 ml/1½ fl oz (3 tablespoons) vegetable stock (broth)

½ ripe honeydew melon

2 small goat's cheeses (each 50 g/2 oz)

½ teaspoon fresh thyme leaves

2 teaspoons maple syrup

1 teaspoon medium strong mustard

1 tablespoon cider vinegar

herb salt

freshly ground pepper

1 teaspoon capers

1 teaspoon walnut oil

2 tablespoons chopped walnuts

Asparagus and strawberry salad

400 g/14 oz green asparagus

salt

sugar

60 ml/2 fl oz (6 tablespoons) strawberry vinegar

60 ml/2 fl oz (6 tablespoons) sunflower oil

freshly ground white pepper

160 g/6 oz fresh strawberries

An unusual combination in which the asparagus and strawberries complement each other's delicate flavours most successfully.

❶ Wash the asparagus, remove the woody ends and cook briefly in boiling water, seasoned with salt, sugar and 5 tablespoons of vinegar. Simmer for 5 minutes over a low heat. Remove the asparagus and rinse in ice cold water to cool them down quickly. Arrange in a flat gratin dish.

❷ Make a marinade with 6 tablespoons of the asparagus water, 1 tablespoon vinegar, oil, salt, pepper and a pinch of sugar. Pour over the asparagus, covering it all with the marinade. Leave to stand.

❸ Clean and wash the strawberries. Purée 40 g/1 1/2 oz strawberries. Cut the remaining ones into quarters and sprinkle with sugar so that the fruit produce a little juice. Mix the strawberry purée and strawberry pieces and add to the asparagus. Stir again.

Serves 4. About 167 kcal per serving

Salad of asparagus tips and mangetouts

500 g/18 oz green asparagus tips

400 g/14 oz mangetouts (snow peas)

250 g/9 oz coloured salad leaves

5 tablespoons olive oil

1 tablespoon balsamic vinegar

salt

freshly ground pepper

80 g/3 oz Parmesan, shaved

watercress for garnish

Mangetouts (snow peas) are a vegetable as delicate as asparagus. Both require very little cooking.

❶ Wash the asparagus tips and cut once lengthways. Wash and prepare the mangetouts (snow peas) and cook together with the asparagus in a small amount of gently boiling water until done.

❷ Wash the salad leaves and arrange on four plates; place the asparagus tips and mangetouts (snow peas) on top. Mix the olive oil, balsamic vinegar, salt and pepper and sprinkle over the salad, asparagus and mangetouts (snow peas).

❸ Slice shavings of Parmesan and sprinkle on the salad, asparagus and mangetouts (snow peas). Garnish with watercress.

Serves 4. About 295 kcal per serving

1/4 celeriac

2 tablespoons lemon juice

250 g/8 oz apples

50 g/2 oz (1/2 cup) walnuts

1 tin of pineapple chunks

4 tablespoons mayonnaise

salt

sugar

freshly ground white pepper

Worcester sauce

6 tablespoons cream

100 g/3 1/2 oz steamed beetroot
  (red beet)

1 bulb chicory

1 orange

salt

freshly ground pepper

1 teaspoon balsamic vinegar

1/2 carton low-fat yoghurt
  (1.5%)

1 teaspoon chopped walnuts

1 slice wholemeal (wholewheat)
  bread

Waldorf salad

The Waldorf salad is one of the most famous of all appetizers making use of apples. As its name suggests, it was created in the Waldorf Astoria Hotel in New York. It is now celebrated throughout the world.

❶ Peel the celeriac and cut into fine strips or grate. Sprinkle immediately with lemon juice. Peel the apples, remove the cores and quarter. Cut the quarters into strips or grate as well. Quarter the walnuts. Mix ingredients carefully together then, drain the pineapple chunks and add them.

❷ Mix the mayonnaise with the salt, sugar, pepper and Worcester sauce. Whip the cream and fold it into the mayonnaise mixture. Season and stir carefully into the salad.

Serves four, 330 kcal per serving

Beetroot (red beet) salad

You can buy ready-cooked beetroot (red beet) in the shops – steamed and vacuum-packed, it has preserved all its important minerals and vitamins such as vitamin C. Combined with oranges and chicory, it makes a delicious salad which is also very filling.

❶ Cut the beetroot (red beet) in half and cut into slices. Divide the leaves of the chicory and arrange them decoratively in a soup plate.

❷ Peel the orange and divide into segments. Arrange the beetroot (red beet) slices on the chicory leaves. Mix salt, pepper, balsamic vinegar and yoghurt together to make a dressing.

❸ Pour the dressing over the vegetables, sprinkle chopped walnuts on top and serve with a slice of wholemeal bread.

Serves 2. About 285 kcal per serving

Power salad

This is a power food for fitness fans. The fruits and vegetables are just packed with vitamins, and the salad can be fitted into any dietary regime. The nutritious mixture of celeriac, apples and carrots supports the body's self-purification system.

1 Wash and peel the carrots, then grate fairly finely. Peel the celeriac and grate that too.

2 Peel the apples, remove the cores and quarter. Cut the quarters into thin slices, sprinkle with lemon juice and sugar.

3 Cut two of the oranges in half and carefully remove the fruit flesh without damaging the skin halves. Peel the remaining oranges. Cut the flesh into small cubes.

4 Mix all the ingredients together, add the sultanas and set aside to marinate for about 20 minutes. Fill the 4 orange skin halves with salad and leave to cool in the refrigerator.

Serves 4. About 210 kcal per serving

500 g/1 lb carrots

100 g/3 1/2 oz celeriac

250 g/8 oz apples

juice of 1 lemon

50 g/2 oz (1/4 cup) brown sugar

4 oranges

50 g/2 oz (1/3 cup) sultanas

One thousand and one nights salad

This is a very special delicacy reminiscent of magical oriental evenings. Redolent of the Orient, this appetizer is a wonderful hors d'oeuvre to have before an exotic main course. Serve it with an aperitif, such as a glass of prosecco with lychee liquor.

700 g/1 1/2 lb untreated eating apples

juice of 1/2 lemon

175 g/6 1/2 oz fresh dates

25 g/1 oz (2 tablespoons) white marzipan

1 teaspoon orange blossom water

4 tablespoons plain yoghurt

4 peeled almonds

4 fresh, green figs

❶ Wash the apples thoroughly, remove the cores and quarter. Cut the quarters into thin julienne strips. Sprinkle with the lemon juice.

❷ Wash the dates, cut in half and remove the stones. Cut into fine strips and mix together in a bowl with the apples.

❸ Put the marzipan, orange blossom water and yoghurt in a bowl and stir to a smooth paste.

❹ Pre-heat oven to 180°C (350°F), Gas Mark 4.

❺ Place the almonds on a baking tray and roast in the pre-heated oven until they are golden brown. Turn occasionally.

❻ Wash the figs, remove the stalks and cut a cross in the top. Press the lower half of the fruit together with thumb and finger to make it open up like a blossom.

❼ Arrange the apple and date mixture on four plates. Place a fig on each one, spoon the yoghurt and orange blossom filling into the middle of each fig, and decorate with a roast almond.

Serves 4. About 240 kcal per serving

Root vegetables with pumpkin seed oil

This salad of fresh root vegetables is ideal as a snack or starter. The root vegetables are grated and served as a salad which will delight all connoisseurs of healthy cuisine. Even the pumpkin seed oil in the dressing is a healthy delicacy because it is rich in trace elements, minerals and vitamins.

❶ Wash, prepare and peel the celeriac, carrots, parsley root and kohlrabi. Using a vegetable grater, grate into thin strips. Put the vegetables in a large bowl.

❷ Mix together the lemon juice, sea salt, multi-coloured pepper and white wine vinegar to make a dressing. Finally, add the pumpkin seed oil and stir carefully with a fork.

❸ Pour the dressing over the raw vegetables and leave to stand for a few minutes. Coarsely chop the cashew nuts and sprinkle over the vegetables. Serve with unleavened bread.

Serves 2. About 114 kcal per serving

1/2 celery root

3 carrots

1 parsley root

1/2 kohlrabi

1 teaspoon lemon juice

sea salt

freshly ground multi-coloured pepper

1 tablespoon white wine vinegar

2 teaspoons pumpkin seed oil

1 tablespoon cashew nuts

Apple and cheese salad

This is a traditional classic among apple salads and should always be present at a party buffet. The protein in the cheese makes this salad an important source of nutrients and energy. Served with a fresh, crusty baguette or ciabatta bread, it will also make a simple, light evening meal.

1 For the dressing: mix the salad cream or mayonnaise, sour cream, lemon juice, vinegar, pepper, salt, sugar and dill in a bowl.

2 Cut the cheese into cubes of 1 cm/1/2 in .

3 Wash the apples thoroughly, remove the cores and quarter. Cut the quarters into fine slices. Carefully mix the cheese and apple slices together in a bowl.

4 Chop the walnuts and sprinkle over the apple and cheese mixture. Serve the dressing in a separate bowl.

Serves four, 590 kcal per serving

4 tablespoons salad cream or
 mayonnaise
125 ml/4 fl oz (1/2 cup) sour
 cream
juice of 1/2 lemon
2 tablespoons vinegar
freshly ground black pepper
salt
sugar
1 tablespoon chopped dill
300 g/10 oz hard cheese
400 g/14 oz untreated red apples
100 g/3 1/2 oz (1 cup) walnuts

Chicory with apples

This chicory and apple salad is a light starter. It is a good idea to soak the chicory leaves briefly in warm water beforehand, to draw out some of the bitterness.

1 Wash the chicory, cut in half and remove the core. Cut crossways into fine strips.

2 Peel the apples, remove the cores and quarter. Grate the apples finely.

3 Mix apples and chicory in a bowl, season with salt and sugar and sprinkle with lemon juice. Add cream to taste if desired.

Serves 4. About 130 kcal per serving

6 chicory buds
700 g/1 1/2 lb apples
salt
sugar
1 tablespoon lemon juice
cream

Tomatoes with tofu (bean curd) and basil dumplings

150 g/5 oz tofu (bean curd)

100 g/3 1/2 in curd cheese

2 cloves garlic

2 spring onions (scallions)

10–12 leaves of basil

3 tablespoons finely chopped walnuts

700 g/1 1/2 lb sliced firm tomatoes

1 tablespoon balsamic vinegar

5 teaspoons olive oil

salt

freshly ground pepper

1/2 teaspoon sugar

The perfect dish for a hot summer's day – a light, refreshing starter (appetizer) which is quick and easy to prepare.

❶ Crumble the tofu (bean curd) finely and mix with the curd cheese. Peel the garlic and spring onions (scallions) and chop finely. Wash the basil and pat it dry. Put a few basil leaves aside for the garnish and finely chop the rest. Add the garlic, spring onions (scallions), basil and walnuts to the tofu (bean curd) and cheese mixture and stir well. Leave to stand briefly.

❷ Wash the tomatoes, remove the stalks, cut into slices and arrange on a dish. Mix together the vinegar, oil, salt, pepper and sugar to make a marinade and pour over the tomatoes. Moisten your hands and roll the prepared mixture into little dumplings. Add them to the tomatoes and garnish with basil leaves.

Serves 4. About 254 kcal per serving

Courgette (zucchini) mousse with tomato salad

It is true that this delicious courgette (zucchini) mousse takes time to prepare but the result is definitely worth it. This exquisite dish is a pleasure to the eye as well as to the palate and therefore makes an ideal party starter (appetizer).

1 Peel the courgettes (zucchini) and cut into small cubes. Sprinkle with salt and put to one side.

2 Put the vegetable stock (broth) in a saucepan and bring to the boil. Add the porridge (rolled) oats and simmer on a very low flame for 30 minutes. Then pour the vegetable stock (broth) through a sieve and reserve the liquid. Put the porridge (rolled) oats to one side.

3 Soften the gelatine in cold water. When ready, take the gelatine out the water and squeeze well. Heat the vegetable stock (broth) again and dissolve the gelatine in it.

4 Put the curd cheese in a large bowl and stir until smooth. Add the vegetable stock (broth), cooled but not yet set, to the curd cheese and stir well to obtain a smooth mixture. Then add the cubed courgettes (zucchini), porridge (rolled) oats, wine vinegar and half the chopped chives to the curd cheese and vegetable stock (broth) mixture. Stir well. Now beat the egg whites and cream separately until stiff. Fold carefully into the curd cheese and vegetable stock (broth) mixture.

5 Rinse six cups in cold water and fill with the courgette (zucchini) mousse. Put in the refrigerator for about 2 hours to set.

6 For the salad, clean and slice the mushrooms, slice the tomatoes and chop the shallots finely.

7 Make a salad dressing with balsamic vinegar, sugar, pepper, salt and vegetable oil. Add the chopped shallots. Divide the tomato and mushroom salad into portions on separate plates, then pour the dressing over. Sprinkle the remaining chives on the salad. Remove the mousse from the cups and put in the centre of each plate, arranging the salad around it.

Serves 6. About 468 kcal per serving

2 large courgettes (zucchini)

salt

300 ml/10 fl oz (1 1/4 cups) vegetable stock (broth)

150 g/5 oz coarse porridge (rolled) oats

8 sheets white gelatine

400 g/14 oz curd cheese

2 tablespoons wine vinegar

1 bunch chives

2 egg white

125 ml/4 fl oz (1/2 cup) cream

300 g/10 oz tomatoes

100 g/3 1/2 oz mushrooms

1 shallot

2 tablespoons balsamic vinegar

sugar

pepper

4 tablespoons vegetable oil

4 eggs

1 bunch smooth parsley

100 g/3 1/2 oz (1 cup) Parmesan

300 g/10 oz courgettes (zucchini)

500 g/18 oz plum tomatoes

3 teaspoons balsamic vinegar

5 teaspoons sunflower oil

1 pinch sugar

salt

red pepper from the mill

100 g/3 1/2 oz rocket

800 g/1 3/4 lb medium tomatoes

120 g/4 oz (1/2 cup) green olives

2 shallots

1/2 bunch basil

2 tablespoons balsamic vinegar

2 tablespoons vegetable stock (broth)

salt

black pepper from the mill

1 teaspoon dried Italian herbs

1 teaspoon honey

4 tablespoons basil-infused oil

2 packs mozzarella (200 g/7 oz each)

4 slices rye bread

Courgette (zucchini) and tomato salad

Courgette (zucchini) and tomato salad is a nourishing, tasty combination of vegetables and eggs which can also be served as a main meal.

❶ Hard-boil (hard cook) the eggs, allow to cool and cut into slices. Coarsely chop the parsley. Grate the Parmesan.

❷ Peel and slice the courgettes (zucchini). Slice the tomatoes. Put the vegetables in a large bowl.

❸ To make the dressing: mix the oil and vinegar, add the sugar and season to taste, stirring well. Pour over the vegetables. Add the sliced eggs and stir very gently.

❹ Sprinkle with parsley and shavings of Parmesan.

Serves 4. About 286 kcal per serving

Tomato and rocket salad

Also known as rucola, rocket is known for giving a "kick" to any salad with its distinctive sharpness.

❶ Tear the rocket into bite-sized pieces. Cut the tomatoes and drained olives into slices. Peel the shallots and dice very finely. Gently mix these ingredients together in a bowl with a few basil leaves.

❷ Pre-heat the oven to 220°C (425°F), Gas mark 7.

❸ For the salad dressing: mix together the vinegar, vegetable stock (broth), salt, pepper, Italian herbs and honey and stir vigorously. Lastly, add the oil. Pour the dressing over the tomato and rocket salad and mix well.

❹ Drain the mozzarella thoroughly, cut into slices and put these on the slices of bread. Sprinkle the remaining basil on the mozzarella and brown under the grill for about 5 minutes.

❺ Serve the tomato and rocket salad with the grilled mozzarella-topped slices of bread.

Serves 4. About 533 kcal per serving

Asparagus salad with artichoke hearts

Artichokes have very large flower heads. These are cut off the plant before they are mature, and the leaves and hairy central core are removed. The part which is eaten is the fleshy heart which remains.

❶ Peel the asparagus, remove the woody ends and cook in boiling water to which sugar and butter have been° added for about 20 minutes until done. Take out of the water, drain and cut into pieces 4 cm/1 1/2 in long.

❷ Drain the artichoke hearts thoroughly and cut in quarters. Wash the tomatoes, remove the stalks (stems) and cut into eight. Wash and prepare the shallots and cut into rings. Add all these ingredients to the asparagus and stir well.

❸ Mix the oil and lemon juice and stir to make a smooth mixture. Season with salt and add to the salad. Sprinkle with finely chopped chives and pepper.

Serves 4. About 188 kcal per serving

500 g/18 oz white asparagus
salt
1 pinch sugar
10 g/3⁄8 oz (2 teaspoons) butter
6 small artichoke hearts
4 firm tomatoes
4 shallots
4 tablespoons lemon juice
5 tablespoons olive oil
1⁄2 bunch chives
freshly ground pepper

Tomato salad with bananas

This red and yellow salad will add an exotic touch to the table. Served in a hollowed-out pineapple, it will conjure up images of the Caribbean.

2 ripe bananas

1 tablespoon lemon juice

500 g/18 oz firm tomatoes

2 tablespoons balsamic vinegar

6 tablespoons sunflower oil

1/2 teaspoon medium strength mustard

salt

pepper

curry powder

sugar

1 bunch smooth parsley

❶ Peel and slice the bananas and sprinkle with lemon juice. Peel the tomatoes, cut in half and slice. Put the tomato and banana slices in a bowl and mix together carefully.

❷ For the salad dressing: mix the vinegar, oil and mustard together and stir vigorously. Season to taste with salt, pepper, curry powder and sugar. Pour the dressing over the salad and stir gently.

❸ Arrange the salad on four plates and sprinkle with chopped parsley.

Serves 4. About 236 kcal per serving

Mixed sprout salad

You can make your own fresh sprouts from germinating grains but you can also buy them ready-made from the health food shop. These crisp sprouts contain a lot of vitamins while they germinate. The spiciest are radish and mustard sprouts.

1 bunch radishes

1 small courgette (zucchini)

1/2 bulb fennel

2 spring onions (scallions)

50 g/2 oz radish sprouts

50 g/2 oz alfalfa sprouts

1 tablespoon lemon juice

freshly ground pepper

1 tablespoon white wine vinegar

1 tablespoon vegetable stock (broth)

1 tablespoon thistle oil

1 small box cress

❶ Wash the radishes, top and tail and cut into slices. Wash, top and tail the courgettes and cut into sticks. Wash the fennel bulbs, top and tail and cut diagonally into fine strips. Wash the spring onions (scallions) and chop into slices. Put all these vegetables in a salad bowl.

❷ Wash the radish and alfalfa sprouts thoroughly and drain. Add to the vegetables in the salad bowl.

❸ Put the lemon juice, pepper, vinegar and stock (broth) in a small bowl and stir to make a smooth mixture. Whisk the thistle oil into this mixture and pour carefully over the vegetables and stir. Allow the salad to stand for 10 minutes. Cut the cress, wash it, dab it dry and sprinkle over the salad.

Serves 2. About 90 kcal per serving

Soups & stews

1 piece pumpkin (about
  200 g/7 oz)

1 potato (50 g/2 oz)

1 onion

1 clove garlic

1 teaspoon sunflower oil

250 ml/8 fl oz (1 cup) vegetable
  stock (broth)

75 ml/3 fl oz (3/8 cup) cream

1 tablespoon crème fraîche

3 teaspoons medium mustard

sea salt

freshly ground white pepper

2 teaspoons pumpkin seed oil

Spicy creamed pumpkin and mustard soup

A real "Halloween" soup, lightly seasoned with mustard and puréed to give it a creamy texture. Hokkaido pumpkins are the best for this purpose because their flesh is very tasty and deep orange in colour. However, this soup can also be prepared with other kinds of pumpkins such as the large garden pumpkin.

❶ Peel the pumpkin, remove the seeds and cut the flesh into dice. Peel the potatoes and cut into cubes. Peel the onion and garlic and chop finely.

❷ Heat the oil in a saucepan and fry the onion until transparent. Add the garlic and fry briefly with the onion. Add the diced pumpkin and potato and continue frying. Pour in the stock (broth), cover and simmer the vegetables for about 15 minutes.

❸ Take two tablespoons of diced pumpkin and put to one side. Add the cream and crème fraîche to the soup and purée with a hand-mixer. Season with mustard, salt and white pepper.

❹ Pour the soup into two bowls, garnish with the diced pumpkin and sprinkle pumpkin seed oil over it.

Serves 2. About 260 kcal per serving

Brussels sprouts and leek soup

Brussels sprouts are a delicious winter vegetable which can be used to make delicious, nutritious soups and soufflés. Served with a slice of wholemeal (wholewheat) bread, this light soup makes a healthy snack or a light meal.

❶ Wash and prepare the Brussels sprouts and cut them into half. Wash and prepare the leeks and celery and cut them into fine strips. Peel the onions and chop finely.

❷ Heat the olive oil in a large saucepan and fry the onion until transparent. Add the vegetables and fry them briefly. Pour in the stock (broth), cover and simmer the vegetables for about 20 minutes over a low heat.

❸ Season the soup with salt, grated nutmeg and freshly ground pepper. Wash the basil, cut the leaves into fine strips and sprinkle over the soup. Pour the soup in two bowls and sprinkle with Parmesan.

Serves 2. About 118 kcal per serving

250 g/9 oz Brussels sprouts
2 leeks
1 stick (stalk) celery
1 onion
1 teaspoon olive oil
400 ml/14 fl oz (1 3⁄4 cups) vegetable stock (broth)
sea salt
freshly grated nutmeg
freshly ground pepper
1 bunch basil
1 tablespoon grated Parmesan

1⁄2 small savoy cabbage or green cabbage
1 kohlrabi
4 large carrots
2 leeks
1⁄2 celeriac
3 sticks (stalks) celery
1⁄4 cauliflower or 1 head of broccoli
1 onion
3 cloves garlic
1⁄2 bunch parsley
2 sprigs thyme
1 bay leaf
1 teaspoon black peppercorns
salt

Vegetable stock (broth)

This vegetarian version of bouillon is the basis for many meals. Other vegetables can be used in addition to the ones mentioned in this recipe. The amounts can also be varied. It is easy to blend the cooked vegetables to a purée with cream.

❶ Wash the vegetables. Depending on the variety, dice, cut into rings or separate into florets.

❷ Put the prepared vegetables, herbs and spices into a large saucepan and cover with cold water.

❸ Simmer the broth uncovered for about 40 minutes, skimming from time to time as necessary. Strain through a sieve and use the vegetables for another recipe.

Serves 4. About 15 kcal per serving

Green (snap) bean and tomato stew

This green (snap) bean and tomato stew is very nourishing and an ideal winter dish. The fragrance of the savory which develops during the cooking makes this dish particularly heart-warming on a cold winter's day.

❶ Peel and slice the onions and garlic. Peel the tomatoes and cut into bite-sized pieces.

❷ Heat the oil in a large saucepan and lightly fry the onions and garlic. Stir in the tomato ketchup. Add the chopped tomatoes and fry briefly.

❸ Drain the green (snap) beans and add to the stew. Add the vegetable stock (broth) and season with vinegar, salt and pepper. Add the savory and bring the mixture to the boil. Reduce the heat and simmer for about 30 minutes, stirring now and again.

❹ When the stew is cooked, remove the savory and season to taste.

Serves 4. About 161 kcal per serving

2 onions

4 cloves garlic

800 g/1 3⁄4 lb beef tomatoes

2 tablespoons olive oil

2 tablespoons tomato ketchup

1 can green (snap) beans
  (400 g/14 oz)

1 litre/1 3⁄4 pints (4 1⁄2 cups)
  vegetable stock (broth)

2 teaspoons balsamic vinegar

salt

white pepper

1 sprig savory

Rocambole garlic cream soup

Spring is the season for rocambole or wild garlic, and wonderful aromatic dishes can be prepared with it. The long sickle-shaped leaves may be found under spreading trees or on the banks of shady streams. Sometimes it can also be bought in street markets.

❶ Wash the spring onions (scallions) and cut into fine rings. Peel the potatoes and cut them into eighths. Melt the butter in a saucepan and sauté the onions and the potatoes for 5 minutes.

❷ Add the vegetable stock (broth) and allow to simmer for 20 to 25 minutes. Purée the soup, stir in the cream and briefly bring to the boil again.

❸ Wash the rocambole, chop it finely and stir it into the soup. Season with salt and freshly ground pepper.

Serves 4. About 240 kcal per serving

3 spring onions (scallions)

3 medium potatoes

2 tablespoons butter

750 ml/1 1⁄4 pints (3 1⁄2 cups)
  vegetable stock (broth)

250 ml/8 fl oz (1 cup) cream

50 g/2 oz rocambole leaves

salt

freshly ground pepper

Coconut and carrot soup

This exquisite soup is a real visual delight and will provide you with large amounts of carotene which converts into the vitally important vitamin A. Because the body can only absorb this vitamin in combination with fat, you should always add a little oil or cream – just a teaspoon is sufficient!

❶ Wash and prepare the spring onions (scallions) and chop them finely. Heat the sunflower oil in a saucepan and fry the spring onions (scallions) lightly. Wash and prepare the carrots, peel and cut into slices. Add the carrots to the onions and fry for a few minutes, stirring constantly.

❷ Sprinkle lemon juice over the carrots, add the vegetable stock (broth) and simmer for about 15 minutes. Purée the vegetables in a blender, add the coconut milk and heat the soup again briefly. If the soup is too thick, add a little more vegetable stock (broth).

❸ Season the soup with curry powder, salt and cayenne pepper. Wash the coriander, chop the leaves coarsely and sprinkle over the soup.

Serves 1. About 118 kcal per serving

1 spring onion (scallion)

1 teaspoon sunflower oil

3 large carrots

1 teaspoon lemon juice

125 ml/4 fl oz (1/2 cup) vegetable stock (broth)

50 ml/1 1/2 fl oz (3 tablespoons) coconut milk

1 pinch curry powder

salt

cayenne pepper

some fresh coriander leaves

Spinach cream soup

You only need a few ingredients for this delicious cream soup. The pine kernels give the soup the necessary extra something and you can be certain it will be praised by your guests.

❶ Heat the butter in a large saucepan. Peel and chop the shallots, then sweat in the butter until transparent. Wash the spinach and add to the shallots. Steam until the spinach collapses slightly.

❷ Add the vegetable stock (broth). Peel the potato and cut into small dice. Add to the soup and simmer for 10 to 15 minutes with the lid on, until the potatoes are done.

❸ Purée the soup and season with grated nutmeg, salt and pepper. Over a very low heat, fold in the crème fraîche. Do not let the soup boil again.

❹ Ladle the soup into bowls, chop the pine kernels and sprinkle them over it. Serve with fresh white bread.

Serves 4. About 250 kcal per serving

1 tablespoon butter

2 shallots

300 g/10 oz fresh spinach

750 ml/1 1/4 pints (3 1/2 cups) vegetable stock (broth)

1 large floury potato

nutmeg

salt

freshly ground white pepper

100 g/3 1/2 oz crème fraîche

50 g/2 oz (3/8 cup) pine kernels

Italian asparagus soup

This Italian recipe is served with croutons or, to use the Italian word, crostini.

1 Wash the asparagus, cut off the woody ends and remove the tips.

2 Heat the oil and butter in a large saucepan. Add the finely chopped onions and braise gently until golden yellow. Add the cut asparagus and cook for a few minutes. Season with salt, add the vegetable stock (broth) and simmer over a low heat for about 1 hour.

3 Strain the asparagus stock (broth) through a sieve into a second saucepan. Rub the asparagus through the sieve, add to the stock (broth) and stir well. Add the asparagus tips. Simmer for another 5 minutes.

4 Sprinkle the soup with finely chopped parsley. Serve with Parmesan and croutons.

Serves 4. About 339 kcal per serving

500 g/18 oz green asparagus

20 g/3⁄4 oz (1 1⁄2 tablespoons) butter

20 ml/1 fl oz (2 tablespoons) olive oil

3 onions

salt

2 litres/3 1⁄2 pints (9 cups) vegetable stock (broth)

1 bunch parsley

100 g/3 1⁄2 oz (1 cup) finely grated Parmesan

croutons

Avocado cream soup

This avocado soup is served hot and should be accompanied by toasted bread. As avocados are very rich, this soup makes a light meal in itself.

1 Halve the avocados, remove the stone (pit), peel and cut the flesh into chunks. Sprinkle immediately with lemon juice to stop them turning brown.

2 Mash the pieces of avocado with a fork and purée them. Put in a saucepan and gradually add the vegetable stock (broth) and white wine, stirring in well. Only add enough liquid to give the soup a creamy consistency.

3 Season the avocado cream with salt and pepper and add the crème fraîche. Bring briefly to the boil. Ladle into soup bowls and serve with croutons as desired.

Serves 4. About 270 kcal per serving

2 ripe avocados

juice of 1 lemon

750 ml/1 1⁄4 pints (3 1⁄2 cups) vegetable stock (broth)

125 ml/4 fl oz (1⁄2 cup) dry white wine

salt

freshly ground white pepper

125 g/4 oz crème fraîche

Mushroom cream soup

Fresh mushrooms are used for this mild, creamy soup. Lots of fresh parsley, some white wine and cream make it a delight for the palate.

❶ Clean the spring onions (scallions) and cut into fine rings. Melt the butter in a large pan and sweat the onions.

❷ Rub the mushrooms with a tea towel, cut into fine slices and sweat them briefly. Dust with flour and stir in. After about 2 minutes, pour the milk over and stir in carefully to avoid lumps.

❸ Add the vegetable stock (broth) and white wine. Simmer for 15 minutes. Purée the soup. Add the cream, bring briefly to the boil again, remove from the heat and add salt, pepper and grated nutmeg to taste.

❹ Wash the parsley and chop finely. Ladle the soup into soup bowls, sprinkle with parsley and serve with croutons.

Serves 4. About 200 kcal per serving

3 spring onions (scallions)

2 tablespoons butter

250 g/8 oz fresh mushrooms

3 tablespoons plain (all purpose) flour

125 ml/4 fl oz (1/2 cup) milk

500 ml/17 fl oz (2 1/4 cups) vegetable stock (broth)

125 ml/4 fl oz (1/2 cup) white wine

125 ml/4 fl oz (1/2 cup) cream

salt

freshly ground white pepper

nutmeg

1 bunch parsley

croutons

Cabbage soup

Cabbage and potatoes make a hearty soup that can stand in for a stew. Leave yourself enough time to cook this soup, about 1 1/2 hours, since the cabbage has to cook slowly.

❶ Cut the cabbage into eighths, wash it and remove the stalk and outer leaves. Cut again lengthways once or twice. Peel the potatoes and kohlrabi and cut into dice of about 3 cm/1 1/4 in.

❷ Peel the onions and chop very fine. Melt butter in a large saucepan and cook the onions gently until they are golden brown. Add the potatoes, cabbage and kohlrabi, pour the vegetable stock (broth) over and simmer on a gentle heat for 1 1/2 hours with the lid on.

❸ Add salt and pepper to taste. Ladle the soup into four large soup plates and serve with thick brown bread.

Serves 4. About 320 kcal per serving

1 kg/2 lb cabbage

500 g/1 lb potatoes

1 kohlrabi

1 onion

1 tablespoon butter

2 litres/3 1/2 pints (9 cups) vegetable stock (broth)

salt

pepper

Paprika and rice soup

Soups should be part of your weekly meal plan – they provide a lot of liquid and very little fat, as well as being quick and easy to prepare. If you add brown rice to the vegetables, this soup becomes a complete meal in itself.

❶ Make a cross-shaped incision in the tomatoes, remove the stalk, blanch briefly in boiling water and peel. Cut the tomatoes into eight pieces. Wash and prepare the peppers and cut into thin strips. Cut the chilli lengthways, remove the seeds and cut into small pieces.

❷ Peel the garlic and onion and chop finely. Heat the olive oil in a large saucepan and fry the garlic and onion until transparent. Add the vegetables and fry briefly with the onion and garlic.

❸ Wash the brown rice and add to the vegetables. Pour in the stock (broth), cover and simmer for about 20–25 minutes over a low heat until the rice is cooked.

❹ Season the soup with salt and pepper. Wash the oregano and chives , chop finely and sprinkle over the soup.

Serves 2. About 215 kcal per serving

2 tomatoes

2 red sweet peppers

1 chilli pepper

1 clove garlic

1 onion

1 tablespoon olive oil

60 g/2 oz (1⁄4 cup) brown rice

1 litre/13⁄4 pints (41⁄2 cups)
   vegetable stock (broth)

salt

freshly ground pepper

some fresh oregano

1 bunch chives

Nettle soup

Young nettles have a subtle, bitter taste and are rich in vitamins. They are also kind to the budget, since you have to pick them yourself. As with spinach, nettles can also be used as a vegetable or a salad.

8 handfuls of young nettles

750 ml/1 1/4 pints (31/2 cups) vegetable stock (broth)

2 shallots

1 clove garlic

2 tablespoons butter

2 tablespoons plain (all purpose) flour

250 ml/8 fl oz (1 cup) milk

2 boiled potatoes

1 tablespoon oil

salt

freshly ground pepper

2 tablespoons sour cream

❶ Wash the nettles and pick them over. Simmer with the vegetable stock (broth) for 7 minutes. Strain through a sieve and set aside the cooking liquid.

❷ Peel the shallots and garlic and chop finely. Sweat in the butter until they become transparent. Dust with flour, sweat briefly and slowly stir in the milk with a balloon whisk.

❸ Add the cooking water from the nettles and simmer for 15 minutes.

❹ Meanwhile, peel and dice the potatoes. Fry in hot oil until golden brown.

❺ Add the nettles to the soup and purée it. Add salt and pepper to taste.

❻ Ladle the soup into bowls. Garnish with the fried, diced potatoes and a swirl of sour cream.

Serves 4. About 240 kcal per serving

Green spelt soup

75 g/3 oz (1/2 cup) green spelt flour

3 tablespoons milk

1 litre/1 3/4 pints (4 1/2 cups) vegetable stock (broth)

1 egg yolk

125 ml/4 fl oz (1/2 cup) cream

salt

pepper

Green spelt is unripe spelt, or German wheat, roasted to enhance its savoury, nutty flavour. It is usually sold as whole grain (groats), but you can sometimes buy it as wholemeal (wholewheat) flour in health food shops.

❶ Mix the green spelt flour with 3 tablespoons of cold milk.

❷ Heat the vegetable stock (broth) and gradually add the mixture of flour and milk. Mix it in carefully with a balloon whisk. Simmer on a gentle heat with the lid on for 25 minutes.

❸ Beat the egg yolk with the cream and stir it into the soup. Do not let it boil again. Season with salt and pepper.

Serves 4. About 160 kcal per serving

Watercress soup

Watercress is appreciated for its piquant taste and its high iron content. You can also make this soup with garden cress.

❶ Wash and pick over the watercress, dry and chop coarsely.

❷ Heat the stock (broth) and milk together in a saucepan. Mix the cornflour (corn starch) to a smooth paste with a little cold water and add it to the saucepan using a balloon whisk. Allow to simmer for 5 minutes. Add lemon juice, salt and pepper to taste.

❸ Mix the cream with the egg yolks. Peel the hard-boiled (hard-cooked) eggs and chop them finely.

❹ Remove the soup from the heat and thicken with the egg and cream mixture.

❺ Put the chopped watercress in soup plates, ladle the soup over it and serve garnished with the chopped egg.

Serves 4. About 230 kcal per serving

1 bunch watercress

750 ml/1 1⁄4 pints (3 1⁄2 cups) vegetable stock (broth)

250 ml/8 fl oz (1 cup) milk

2 level tablespoons cornflour (corn starch)

juice of 1⁄2 lemon

salt

freshly ground white pepper

100 ml/3 1⁄2 fl oz (1⁄2 cup) cream

2 egg yolks

2 hard-boiled (hard-cooked) eggs

Pumpkin soup

In the autumn markets, pumpkins glow orange in all sizes from enormous to the small and handy. The most aromatic are the musk pumpkins or the little Hokaidos. This versatile vegetable is easy to keep all winter and it is used here in a sweet soup which will also be popular with children.

❶ Peel the pumpkin, scrape out the seeds and dice the flesh. Cover with 250 ml/8 fl oz (1 cup) water and cook it for 30 minutes until soft. Purée with a hand blender or in a blender.

❷ Heat the milk, add the rice and let it swell over a gentle heat. Add the puréed pumpkin.

❸ Stir in the almonds. Add salt and rose water to taste. Serve with sugar, cinnamon and a swirl of sour cream.

Serves 4. About 240 kcal per serving

500 g/1 lb pumpkin

500 ml/17 fl oz (2 1⁄4 cups) milk

40 g/1 1⁄2 oz (3⁄8 cup) short-grain pudding rice

50 g/2 oz (3⁄8 cup) ground almonds

salt

2 tablespoons rose water

cinnamon

sugar

4 tablespoons sour cream

Herb cream soup

Total of 150 g/6 oz fresh herbs (for instance, chervil, tarragon, parsley, chives, sorrel, dill, watercress or lemon balm)

1 tablespoon lemon juice

3 spring onions (scallions)

1 tablespoon butter

1 tablespoon cornflour (corn starch)

500 ml/17 fl oz (2 1/4 cups) vegetable stock (broth)

125 ml/4 fl oz (1/2 cup) white wine

125 ml/4 fl oz (1/2 cup) cream

salt

pepper

nutmeg

The herbs that are available at the time will determine which ones used for this soup. There should be at least four different kinds, so that the soup is really aromatic. The basis is a delicate vegetable stock (broth), refined with cream towards the end of the cooking time.

❶ Wash the herbs, dry them with a tea towel and remove the stalks. Chop finely on a large board and sprinkle with lemon juice.

❷ Clean the spring onions (scallions) and cut into fine rings. Heat the butter in a saucepan and sauté the onions. Dust with cornflour (corn starch) and add the vegetable stock (broth), stirring carefully to avoid lumps.

❸ Add the white wine and cream and simmer for a few minutes. Add the chopped herbs and leave to steep for 5 minutes, but be careful not to boil it again.

❹ Season the soup with salt, pepper and grated nutmeg and serve with croutons.

Serves 4. About 180 kcal per serving

Brown potato soup

Potato soup is very popular and there are countless versions of it. For the typical potato taste, it is important to use a good variety of potato. In this old recipe, the soup has a nice dark colour because all the ingredients are evenly browned.

1 Scrub the potatoes under running water, peel and dice. Peel the vegetables and onion. Cut them up small. Melt the clarified butter and brown the vegetables, onion and potatoes evenly over a medium heat.

2 Add the stock (broth). Scrape the bottom of the saucepan with a wooden spoon to free any browned material, add the bay leaf, cover and cook for 40 minutes.

3 Purée the soup with a hand blender or in a blender and stir in the crème fraîche. Season with salt and pepper to taste. Sprinkle with parsley before serving

Serves 4. About 310 kcal per serving

500 g/1 lb floury potatoes

1/4 celeriac

1 parsnip

1 small onion

50 g/2 oz (4 tablespoons) clarified butter

1 litre/1 3⁄4 pints (4 1⁄2 cups) vegetable stock (broth)

1 bay leaf

100 g/3 1⁄2 oz crème fraîche

salt

freshly ground pepper

2 tablespoons chopped parsley

Milk soup

For this soup little pasta-like dumplings are made from rye flour, cheese and water, cooked in the milk. They give the soup a creamy consistency.

1 Knead the rye flour with the grated cheese and 3 to 4 tablespoons water into a firm dough. If the dough is too crumbly, add a little more water.

2 Refrigerate the dough for 15 minutes, then roll it out on a wooden board and cut into short noodles with a knife.

3 Bring the milk, buttermilk and salt to the boil, add the noodles and leave to steep over low heat for 5 minutes until they are done. Add salt, pepper and grated nutmeg to the milk soup to taste.

Serves 4. About 160 kcal per serving

70 g/3 oz (3⁄4cup) rye flour

50 g/2 oz (1/2 cup) grated Emmental cheese

500 ml/17 fl oz (2 1⁄4 cups) milk

500 ml/17 fl oz (2 1⁄4 cups) buttermilk

salt

freshly ground white pepper

nutmeg

5 onions

4 tablespoons olive oil

50 g/2 oz (3⁄8 cup) pine kernels

1 teaspoon coarse sea salt

several leaves fresh sweet basil

2 cloves garlic

250 g/8 oz courgettes (zucchini)

250 g/8 oz aubergines (eggplants)

1 large red sweet (bell) pepper

250 g/8 oz tomatoes

1 bay leaf

15 peppercorns

2 sprigs fresh thyme

2 sprigs fresh rosemary

2 sprigs fresh oregano

(as an alternative to the fresh
    herbs, 1 tablespoon herbes de
    Provence)

250 ml/8 fl oz (1 cup) dry white
    wine

salt

freshly ground pepper

Mediterranean vegetable soup

The charcteristic ingredients of the cuisine of the south make this soup a perfect summer meal. It should be served well-chilled with crunchy slices of baguette and a dry white wine – the one you have used for the soup would be ideal.

❶ Peel and chop the onions. Heat the oil in a large saucepan and sweat the onions until transparent. Grind the pine kernels, sea salt, sweet basil and peeled garlic with a pestle and mortar and add to the onions.

❷ Wash the courgettes (zucchini), aubergines (eggplants), sweet (bell) peppers and tomatoes and cut into 2 cm/1 in pieces. Put in the pan and sweat briefly.

❸ Put the herbs and spices in a little muslin bag (or a tea ball) and add to the vegetables in the pan. Add the white wine and simmer for 20 minutes with the lid on.

❹ Remove the bag of spices, purée the soup and pass it through a fine sieve. Add salt and freshly ground pepper to taste and set aside to cool for 2 hours.

Serves 4. About 280 kcal per serving

Leek soup with saffron

This soup combines two interesting aromas and is very striking with the glowing orange-yellow of the saffron. It can be served as a starter.

1 Wash the leeks and cut the white and light green parts (only) into rings. Peel and dice the potatoes.

2 Blanch one-third of the leek rings in boiling salted water until just done and plunge into cold water. Drain in a colander. Peel and crush the garlic.

3 Heat the oil in a saucepan and sweat the rest of the leek with the potatoes and garlic, but do not let them brown. Add the stock (broth) and simmer for 20 minutes.

4 Meanwhile, make the saffron sauce. Heat the butter until it begins to sizzle in a small pan. Add the blanched leek and the saffron strands, and pour in 4 tablespoons of water.

5 Purée the soup. Stir in the crème fraîche and add salt, pepper and freshly grated nutmeg to taste.

6 Ladle the soup into warmed soup plates, garnish with the leek rings and a swirl of the saffron sauce.

Serves 4. About 240 kcal per serving

2 large leeks

250 g/8 oz floury potatoes

salt

1 clove of garlic

2 tablespoons oil

750 ml/1 1/4 pints (3 1/2 cups) vegetable stock (broth)

30 g/1 oz (2 tablespoons) butter

1/2 teaspoon saffron strands

2 tablespoons crème fraîche

salt

freshly ground white pepper

nutmeg

Sorrel soup

You can pick this wild-growing herb with its slightly bitter taste your-self in the spring, or it can sometimes be bought from the greengrocer.

250 g/8 oz sorrel

25 g butter

100 ml/3 1/2 fl oz (1/2 cup) dry white wine

500 ml/17 fl oz (2 1/4 cups) vegatable stock (broth)

2 boiled potatoes, peeled

100 g/3 1/2 oz crème fraîche

freshly ground white pepper

salt

❶ Wash and pick over the sorrel. Dry it and cut into fine strips.

❷ Melt the butter in a saucepan. Add two-thirds of the sorrel, all the wine and the vegetable stock (broth) and simmer for 7 minutes. Dice the potatoes and add to the soup. Purée the soup and pass it through a sieve.

❸ Stir the crème fraîche into the soup, adding salt and pepper to taste. Re-heat the soup briefly and garnish with the remaining strips of sorrel.

Serves 4. About 230 kcal per serving

Chervil soup

Chervil soup is traditionally eaten in Bavaria on Maundy Thursday. It should always be made using fresh chervil and can be refined with cream or crème fraîche.

2 spring onions (scallions)

50 g/2 oz (4 tablespoons) butter

2 tablespoons cornflour (corn starch)

1 litre/1 3/4 pints (4 1/2 cups) vegetable stock (broth)

1 large bunch chervil

salt

freshly ground white pepper

if desired, 100 ml/3 1/2 fl oz (1/2 cup) cream or 2 tablespoons crème fraîche

❶ Wash the spring onions (scallions) and cut into fine rings. Heat the butter in a large saucepan and sweat the onions. Dust with the cornflower (corn starch) and brown for several minutes.

❷ Add the vegetable stock (broth), beat with a balloon whisk and simmer for 30 minutes. Wash the chervil, setting a few sprigs aside for the garnish. Remove the stalks from the remaining sprigs and chop fine.

❸ Add the chervil to the soup, simmer for 10 minutes, then stir in the cream or crème fraîche as desired. Keep the soup warm but be careful not to boil it again.

❹ Add salt and pepper to taste, ladle into soup bowls and garnish with the sprigs of chervil.

Serves 4. About 230 kcal per serving

Gazpacho

The Spanish speciality gazpacho is a refreshing vegetable soup which is served ice-cold. It can also be diluted with ice-cold water. The soup is eaten with croutons, diced cucumber, red peppers, tomatoes and onions served in bowls on the table.

800 g/1 3⁄4 lb ripe tomatoes

2 onions

2–3 cloves garlic

1 cucumber

1 green pepper

1 red pepper

3 tablespoons olive oil

1 tablespoon wine vinegar

salt

freshly ground pepper

2–3 slices white bread, crusts removed

25 g/1 oz (2 tablespoons) butter

❶ Peel and quarter the tomatoes and remove the seeds. Peel the onions and garlic. Peel the cucumber and cut in half lengthways; remove the seeds and dice. Cut the red pepper in half, remove the seeds and cut into eight pieces.

❷ Cut one-third of the tomatoes, onions, garlic, cucumber and red pepper into small cubes. Purée the rest in the blender with oil and vinegar and season with salt and pepper. Pour the gazpacho in a bowl, cover and put in the refrigerator.

❸ Just before serving, cut slices of white bread into small cubes. Heat some butter in a pan and fry the bread cubes until golden brown. Put in a small bowl like the other diced vegetables and serve with the soup.

Serves 4. About 250 kcal per serving

Porcini and tortellini soup

Fresh porcini (also known as ceps, yellow boletus or Italian muhrooms) give this soup a wonderful flavour. If fresh porcini are not available, dry ones can be used instead. They must be soaked in cold water for 2 hours before cooking.

4 small firm porcini

2 shallots

1 tablespoon butter

1 litre/1 3⁄4 pints (4 1⁄2 cups) vegetable stock (broth)

150 g/5 oz fresh tortellini, filled with cheese

1 bunch chervil

❶ Wash the porcini and cut into fine slices. Cut the slices into tiny cubes. Peel the shallots and chop small.

❷ Melt the butter in a large saucepan, cook the shallots gently until transparent, add the mushrooms and sauté.

❸ Pour in the vegetable stock (broth) and simmer for 2 minutes. Add the tortellini and cook in the stock (broth) for 5 minutes. They should still be firm to the bite. Wash and finely chop the chervil, adding it to the hot soup. Serve in large soup plates.

Serves 4. About 150 kcal per serving

Carrot cream soup

Delicately mild and faintly sweet in flavour, this cream of carrot soup with potatoes is a real delight for the palate. When rounded off with crème fraîche, the aroma of the soup unfolds itself to perfection.

❶ Melt the butter in a large saucepant. Peel and chop the shallots, then sweat in the butter until transparent.

❷ Peel and dice the carrots and potatoes, add to the shallots and sweat them too. Add the vegetable stock (broth) and the milk and simmer for 20 minutes on a gentle heat with the lid on.

❸ Remove the soup from the heat, purée it and stir in the crème fraîche. If the soup is too thick, add a little more milk and bring to the boil again. Add salt, pepper, some grated nutmeg and the orange juice to taste.

❹ Wash the parsley, remove the stalks and chop it finely. Ladle the soup into soup plates, sprinkle over the parsley and serve with the croutons.

Serves 4. About 270 kcal per serving

2 tablespoons butter

2 shallots

500 g/1 lb carrots

200 g/7 oz floury potatoes

750 ml/1 1/4 pints (3 1/2 cups) vegetable stock (broth)

250 ml/8 fl oz (1 cup) milk

125 g/4 oz crème fraîche

salt

freshly ground white pepper

nutmeg

juice of 1 orange

1 bunch flat-leaf parsley

croutons

Peanut soup

3 shallots

3 spring onions (scallions)

1 tablespoon butter

1 tablespoon tomato puree

chilli powder

salt

750 ml/1 1/4 pints (3 1/2 cups)
vegetable stock (broth)

5 tablespoons peanut butter

3 tablespoons coconut milk

freshly ground white pepper

1 tablespoon lemon juice

The original recipe for this unusual and delicious soup comes from west Africa. Peanuts are grown there, from which a variety of sweet and savoury dishes are made. The tangy flavour of the soup comes from the use of chilli powder and lemon juice.

❶ Peel and finely chop the shallots and spring onions (scallions). Melt butter in a large casserole dish and fry the onions until lightly golden.

❷ Mix in the tomato puree and season with a little chilli and salt. Add 250 ml/8 fl oz (1 cup) of the stock (broth) and simmer for 10 minutes.

❸ Remove the soup from heat and liquidize. Add the rest of the stock (broth) and heat again gently. Gradually add the peanut butter to the hot soup with a spoon and then beat thoroughly.

❹ Finally add the coconut milk and let the soup simmer gently for a few minutes. Season with salt, freshly ground pepper and lemon juice.

Serves 4. About 200 kcal per serving

Lemon rice soup

1 litre/1 3/4 pints (4 1/2 cups)
vegetable stock (broth)

juice of 2 lemons

2 stalks lemongrass

2 spring onions (scallions)

4 tablespoons basmati rice

1 teaspoon sugar

1 tablespoon dry sherry

salt

pepper

soy sauce

zest of 1 unsprayed lemon

1 whole unsprayed lemon

several mint leaves

Reminiscent of Asian cuisine, this is a very light and fragrant soup. It is made with unsprayed lemons and rice and should be served piping hot. Serve it with white bread.

❶ Bring the vegetable stock (broth) and lemon juice to the boil in a large saucepan. Beat the lemongrass stalks to flatten them slightly and add to the stock (broth). Clean the spring onions (scallions), cut into fine rings and add them.

❷ Wash the rice and stir into the boiling soup. Reduce the heat and simmer for 20 minutes with the lid on. Remove the lemongrass stalks.

❸ Add sugar, sherry, salt, pepper and a dash of soy sauce for a piquant flavour. Add the lemon zest and leave the soup to steep for another 3 to 4 minutes.

❹ Wash the whole lemon and cut it into eight segments. Ladle the soup into Asian soup bowls and garnish with the lemon segments and the mint leaves.

Serves 4. About 70 kcal per serving

Artichoke soup

Artichoke soup goes perfectly with an Italian menu. If you cannot find any fresh artichokes, the marinated kind will do as well. In this case the cooking time is reduced by 10 minutes.

1 Wash the artichoke hearts and cut off the hard tops. Peel and quarter the onions. Melt the butter in a large saucepan and sweat the onions.

2 Add 10 of the artichoke hearts, sprinkle with lemon juice and cook for 5 minutes. Add the vegetable stock (broth) and simmer the soup for 20 minutes. Remove the pan from heat, purée the soup and pass it through a fine sieve.

3 Season with salt and pepper to taste. Add the cream and bring briefly to the boil again.

4 Sprinkle on the artichokes with parmesan and brown quickly under the grill. Ladle the soup into soup plates and garnish each with a artichoke heart.

Serves 4. About 320 kcal per serving

10 artichoke hearts

2 onions

40 g/1 1/2 oz (3 tablespoons) butter

juice of 1/2 lemon

1 litre/1 3/4 pints (4 1/2 cups) vegetable stock (broth)

salt

pepper

250 ml/8 fl oz (1 cup) cream

4 artichoke hearts for garnish

grated parmesan

Cold summer soup

This puréed soup is deliciously refreshing on a hot summer day and awakens memories of holidays in Provence. You can also serve finely diced raw vegetables and croutons with the soup.

❶ Peel and finely dice the shallots. Peel and crush the garlic. Wash and prepare the vegetables, cutting them into small pieces.

❷ Heat the olive oil in a saucepan and sweat the shallots and garlic. Add the vegetables and brown lightly.

❸ Add all the herbs except the sweet basil and add the wine and stock (broth). Simmer gently for 20 minutes.

❹ Remove the herbs, purée the soup and pass through a sieve. Set aside to cool before serving Wash the basil, tear the leaves into small strips and use them to garnish the soup when it is cool.

Serves 4. About 220 kcal per serving

5 shallots

3 cloves garlic

2 small courgettes (zucchini)

1 eggplant

1 red sweet (bell) pepper

2 tomatoes

5 tablespoons olive oil

1 bay leaf

2 sprigs thyme

1 sprig rosemary

250 ml/8 fl oz (1 cup) dry white wine

250 ml/8 fl oz (1 cup) vegetable stock (broth)

salt

freshly ground pepper

1 bunch sweet basil

Minestrone

Every Italian housewife has her own recipe for minestrone. The main ingredients in this traditional soup consist of a variety of vegetables, pulses, tomatoes and rice or pasta. The soup develops even more taste when reheated. It's also well worth trying out chilled minestrone in summer.

200 g/7 oz (1 1/4 cups) dried beans

1 onion

2 cloves garlic

2 carrots

3 celery sticks (stalks)

2 courgettes (zucchini)

1 leek

2 potatoes

3 large tomatoes

2 tablespoons olive oil

2 litres/3 1/2 pints (9 cups) of vegetable stock (broth)

1 bayleaf

2 sprigs thyme

freshly ground pepper

salt

125 g/4 oz durum wheat small noodles

6 tablespoons grated parmesan

3 tablespoons chopped parsley

❶ Soak the beans overnight in cold water, then drain and leave to dry.

❷ Peel the onion and garlic, chopping the onion finely and pressing the garlic. Peel the carrots, wash the celery, and cut both into slices. Wash and dice the courgette (zucchini). Wash the leek and cut into rings. Peel the potatoes and cut into cubes of 1 cm/1/2 in. Pour boiling water over the tomatoes, then peel, remove seeds and chop.

❸ Heat the olive oil in a pan. Add the onion and garlic and fry until transparent. Add the beans and all the remaining vegetables except for the tomatoes and simmer briefly.

❹ Add the tomatoes and stock (broth), together with the herbs. Simmer gently on a low heat for about 2 hours. Add the pasta towards the end of the cooking time, according to the instructions on the packet.

❺ Season the soup to taste and serve sprinkled with parmesan and parsley.

Serves 6. About 420 kcal per serving

Sweet (bell) pepper soup

Ripe sweet (bell) peppers give this red, creamy soup a fruity flavor, while oregano, garlic and freshly milled coloured pepper round off the taste to perfection.

5 red sweet (bell) peppers

1 hot red chili pepper

1 tablespoon olive oil

2 cloves garlic

2 onions

5 tomatoes

1 litre/1 3⁄4 pints (4 1/2 cups) vegetable stock (broth)

salt

coarsely ground coloured pepper

fresh oregano

❶ Wash and quarter the peppers, remove the white pith and seeds and put skin side up on a grill rack. Cook for 10 to 15 minutes at 200°C (400°F), Gas Mark 6, until the skin shows signs of blistering. Remove from the oven, put in a plastic bag and seal it, then leave for 5 minutes. Take out again and peel. Set aside.

❷ Wash the chili pepper and cut into fine rings. Heat the olive oil and sweat the pepper over a low heat. Peel and finely chop the garlic and the onions, add to the chili pepper and sauté until transparent.

❸ Pour boiling water over the tomatoes and peel them. Chop and add to the onions and chili pepper. Simmer for about 5 minutes until soft,then add the bell peppers. Purée.

❹ Put the tomato and pepper sauce in a large saucepan, add the vegetable stock (broth) and cook over a low heat for 5 minutes. Add salt and pepper. Sprinkle finely chopped oregano over the soup to taste. Serve with fresh white bread.

Serves 4. About 70 kcal per serving

South Tyrolean chestnut soup

The South Tyrol is celebrated for the plentiful harvest of nuts from its sweet chestnut trees each autumn. This has given rise to many local dishes in which the nutritious sweet chestnut plays an important role.

1 Cut a cross in the top of each chestnut with a sharp knife and put them on a baking sheet. Bake in a preheated oven at 200°C (400°F), Gas Mark 6, for about 15 minutes until the skins splits open.

2 Peel the hot chestnuts immediately. Heat the stock (broth), add the chestnuts and simmer for 15 minutes. Blend the chestnuts and stock (broth) with a hand blender, then add the white wine and salt and pepper.

3 Add the cream to the soup and bring quickly to the boil. Remove the soup from the heat. Wash the chervil and chop finely before stirring it in. Pour the chestnut soup into soup bowls and decorate with croutons.

Serves 4. About 240 kcal per serving

300 g/10 oz sweet chestnuts

1 litre/1 3⁄4 pints (4 1⁄2 cups) vegetable stock (broth)

125 ml/4 fl oz (1⁄2 cup) dry white wine

salt

freshly ground white pepper

125 ml/4 fl oz (1⁄2 cup) cream

1 bunch chervil

Bread soup

Delicious soups can be made using bread from the day before. No-one would think that they are made from leftovers. There are many variations; in this Bavarian version, fried onion rings give the soup a hearty flavour.

1 Peel the onions and cut into fine rings. Melt the butter in a pan and fry the onions slowly to a golden brown.

2 Arrange the onion rings on the bread slices and sprinkle on the grated cheese. Put in the oven for 5 minutes at 180°C (350°F), Gas Mark 4, to melt the cheese. Bring the vegetable stock (broth) to the boil.

3 Lay the bread with the melted cheese in soup plates. Pour in the soup slowly from the edge so that the slices are barely covered and soak up the broth slowly from underneath.

4 Wash the chives and chop into little rings. Sprinkle them over the soup with the freshly ground pepper. Add salt to taste.

Serves 4. About 260 kcal per serving

2 onions

3 tablespoons butter

4 slices stale black bread

100 g/3 1⁄2 oz (1 cup) finely grated Emmental cheese

1 litre/1 3⁄4 pints (4 1⁄2 cups) vegetable stock (broth)

freshly ground white pepper

1⁄2 bunch chives

salt

Vegetables

1 aubergine (eggplant)

1 courgette (zucchini)

2 potatoes

100 g/3 1/2 oz broccoli

2 carrots

sea salt

2 onions

1 clove garlic

1 teaspoon olive oil

150 g/5 oz low-fat yoghurt
(1.5%)

1 egg

1 tablespoon dried herbs of
Provence

freshly ground pepper

30 g/1 oz low-fat hard cheese

Aubergine (eggplant) gratin

Aubergines (eggplants) absorb a lot of oil while cooking, whether fried, baked or grilled. However, in this recipe they are cooked with other vegetables in a little salted water without any fat, then gratiné with a yoghurt sauce and cheese.

❶ Wash and prepare the courgettes and aubergine and cut into slices about 1 cm/3/8 in thick. Peel the potatoes and cut them into slices of the same thickness. Wash the broccoli and divide into florets. Peel the carrots and cut into thick sticks.

❷ Heat 125 ml/4 fl oz (1/2 cup) water in a large saucepan, season with a little salt and add the vegetables. Cover and simmer over a low heat for about 10 minutes.

❸ Peel the onions and garlic and chop finely. Heat the olive oil in a small pan and fry the onions and garlic until transparent. Drain the aubergine (eggplant) and courgette (zucchini) slices and reserve the cooking liquid. Arrange them with the onion and garlic mixture in alternate layers in the gratin dish.

❹ Pre-heat the oven to 180°C (350°F), Gas mark 4.

❺ Add the egg, 3 tablespoons of the reserved cooking liquid, the herbs of Provence , salt and pepper to the yoghurt, stir well and pour over the vegetables. Grate the cheese and sprinkle on top. Bake the gratin in the oven for about 20–25 minutes.

Serves 2. About 265 kcal per serving

Chop Suey

This dish can be varied according to taste and mood. Whatever the choice, the most important ingredient in chop suey are the bean sprouts which must be served immediately after cooking because they do not remain crisp for long.

1 Wash and prepare the celery and pepper. Remove the seeds from the pepper. Peel the onions. Rub the mushrooms clean with kitchen paper. Cut all the vegetables into thin strips.

2 Put the cornflour (corn starch) in a small bowl. Add the soy sauce, sherry and 1 tablespoon water, stir to obtain a smooth mixture and leave to stand briefly.

3 Heat the sesame oil in a wok or large pan. Add the vegetables and fry for about 5 minutes, stirring continuously. The vegetables must be cooked but still crisp.

4 Wash the bean sprouts, dab dry and add to the vegetables. Cook for another minute.

5 Stir the cornflour (corn starch) mixture briefly again and add slowly to the vegetables in the pan. Bring quickly to the boil, stirring continuously. Simmer for 2 more minutes over a low heat while stirring. Season with salt and pepper and serve immediately.

Serves 2. About 175 kcal per serving.

1/2 stick (stalk) celery

1/2 red sweet pepper

1/2 onion

2 mushrooms

1 teaspoon cornflour (corn starch)

1 tablespoon soy sauce

2 teaspoons sherry

11/2 tablespoons sesame oil

100 g/3 1/2 oz mung bean sprouts

75 g/3 oz soya bean sprouts

salt

freshly ground pepper

Kohlrabi gratin with wild garlic sauce

Wild garlic has a spicy, aromatic flavour and it can be bought fresh in markets in the spring. In other seasons when it is not available it can be replaced by chives.

❶ Peel the kohlrabi and potatoes and cut into slices 1 cm/3⁄8 in thick. Heat the stock (broth) in a saucepan, add the potato and kohlrabi slices, cover and cook for about 15 minutes until ready.

❷ Remove the potatoes and kohlrabi from the water, drain well and put in a gratin dish. Season with salt, pepper and freshly grated nutmeg. Wash the wild garlic, chop finely and add together with the egg to the yoghurt. Stir well until smooth and pour over the vegetables.

❸ Pre-heat the oven to 180°C (350°F), Gas mark 4. Grate the cheese and sprinkle with the sunflower seeds over the gratin. Bake in the oven for about 10 minutes.

Serves 2. About 310 kcal per serving

3 kohlrabi

3 potatoes

250 ml/8 fl oz (1 cup) vegetable stock (broth)

salt

freshly ground pepper

some grated nutmeg

125 g/4 1⁄2 oz low-fat yoghurt (1.5%)

1 egg

1 bunch wild garlic

30 g/1 oz low-fat hard cheese

1 tablespoon sunflower seeds

50 g/2 oz shelled walnuts

2 medium courgettes (zucchini)

100 g/3 1⁄2 oz fromage frais with yoghurt

2 tablespoons low-fat milk (1.5%)

herb salt

freshly ground pepper

1 pinch cayenne pepper

1 tomato

olive oil for the dish

1 tablespoon chopped parsley

Courgettes (zucchini) with walnut filling

Courgettes (zucchini) are a very versatile member of the pumpkin family and they are available throughout the year. Garlic fans can enhance the flavour of the fromage frais by adding a crushed clove of garlic.

❶ Pre-heat the oven to 180°C (350°F), Gas mark 4. Coarsely chop the walnuts. Wash and prepare the courgettes (zucchini) and cut in half lengthways. Scoop out the flesh with a teaspoon and cut it into small cubes.

❷ Mix the fromage frais and milk and stir to make a smooth mixture. Season with herb salt, pepper and cayenne. Wash the tomatoes, remove the stalks and cut into dice. Add to the fromage frais with the diced courgettes (zucchini) and chopped walnuts. Stir well and check the seasoning again.

❸ Grease an ovenproof dish with olive oil and place the hollowed-out courgette (zucchini) halves in it. Fill them with the fromage frais mixture. Bake in the oven for about 30 minutes. Sprinkle with parsley and serve hot with unleavened bread.

Serves 2. About 270 kcal per serving

Red cabbage with apples

This is a sweet-and-sour dish, with the mixture of red wine vinegar and sugar giving it a distinctive flavour. Served with potatoes or "Spätzle" it makes a delicious vegetarian meal.

1 Peel the onions and cut into fine rings. Peel the apples, quarter and core. Cut the quarters into fine slices. Wash and halve the red cabbage. Cut it into thin strips.

2 Heat the vegetable oil in a heavy saucepan and sauté the onions over a medium heat until golden brown. Stir in the apples and sauté for another 2 to 3 minutes.

3 Add the cabbage, red wine vinegar, red wine, sugar, cloves, mustard seed, raisins and spices. Bring slowly to the boil over a medium heat while stirring occasionally.

4 Cover the saucepan and allow everything to simmer for 40 minutes until the cabbage is soft and the liquid has cooked away. Stir from time to time. If it gets too dry, add a little water. Stir in the redcurrant jelly just before serving.

Serves 4. About 320 kcal per serving

2 onions
250 g/1/2 lb eating apples
2 kg/4 lb red cabbage
2 tablespoons vegetable oil
4 tablespoons red wine vinegar
125 ml/4 fl oz (1/2 cup) red wine
2 tablespoons sugar
1/4 teaspoon ground cloves
1 to 2 teaspoons mustard seed
50 g/2 oz (1/3 cup) raisins
salt
freshly ground black pepper
1 to 2 tablespoons redcurrant jelly

400 g/14 oz small waxy potatoes

250 g/9 oz carrots

1 onion

1 tablespoon olive oil

1 tablespoon sesame seeds

salt

freshly ground black pepper

some fresh oregano leaves

Potato and carrot fricassée

Even fried potatoes can be prepared with very little fat. First they are steamed, then fried with the carrots in a non-stick pan using very little fat.

1 Clean the potatoes with a brush under the tap and put in a steamer. Peel the carrots and cut into quarters lengthways. Fill the steamer with about 250 ml/8 fl oz (1 cup) water – the water must not reach up to the vegetables – and bring to the boil. Steam the carrots and potatoes for about 20–25 minutes and check if they are cooked enough.

2 Peel the potatoes and cut into slices. Peel the onions and cut into rings. Heat the olive oil in a large non-stick pan, add the onions and fry. Add the sesame seeds and fry briefly.

3 Add the carrots and potatoes and fry slowly in the oil, gently turning several times. Season with salt, freshly ground pepper and fresh oregano.

Serves 2. About 260 kcal per serving

2 onions

2 small courgettes (zucchini)

75 g/3 oz small mushrooms

1 red sweet pepper

125 ml/4 fl oz (1/2 cup) vegetable
stock (broth)

2 teaspoons groundnut oil

freshly ground pepper

juice of 1 lemon

2 metal or wood skewers

for the dip:

5 tablespoons tomato ketchup
(catsup)

1 tablespoon low-fat salad cream

1 clove garlic

1 pinch chilli pepper

1/2 bunch coriander

Vegetable kebabs
with a spicy dip

You can use almost any vegetable in this recipe, depending on what is available at the time. Cooking the vegetables in the vegetable stock (broth) before grilling them is a useful way of ensuring that the vegetables are cooked enough.

1 Peel and halve the onions. Wash and prepare the courgettes (zucchini) and cut into slices 2 cm/3⁄4 in thick . Cut the woody ends off the mushrooms and rub clean with kitchen paper. Cut the pepper into four pieces, remove the stalk and seeds and cut into strips 2 cm/3⁄4 in wide.

2 Heat the vegetable stock (broth) in a large saucepan, add the vegetables, cover and cook over a medium heat for about 10 minutes.

3 Pre-heat the oven to 180°C (350°F), Gas mark 4.

4 Remove the vegetables from the saucepan and drain well. Thread the onion halves, slices of courgette, strips of pepper and whole mushrooms in rotation on long metal or wooden skewers. Brush with oil. Grill for 10–15 minutes. Season with freshly ground pepper and sprinkle with lemon juice.

5 For the dip, mix the tomato ketchup (catsup) and salad cream together. Peel the garlic and chop finely. Wash the coriander, pat dry and chop the leaves finely. Stir into the sauce. Season the dip with chilli powder and serve with the kebabs.

Serves 2. About 200 kcal per serving

Caribbean vegetable stew

The more exotic ingredients in this Caribbean dish such as the okra, chillies, limes, coconut milk and fresh coriander are available in shops specialising in eastern and Caribbean food. The inhabitants of the Caribbean prefer the very hottest chillies but this is not recommended for beginners!

250 g/9 oz fresh leaf spinach

60 g/2 oz okra

1 small aubergine (eggplant)

2 shallots

1 clove garlic

1 mild red chilli pepper

1 teaspoon olive oil

200 ml/7 fl oz (7/8 cup) vegetable stock (broth)

1 teaspoon fresh thyme leaves

1 pinch ground allspice

1 teaspoon lime juice

125 ml/4 fl oz (1/2 cup) coconut milk (from the can)

75 ml low-fat milk (1.5%)

sea salt

freshly ground pepper

1 tablespoon chopped green coriander

❶ Remove any damaged leaves and thick stalks from the spinach and wash. Wash and prepare the okra and aubergine, and cut the latter into dice. Peel the shallots and garlic and chop finely. Remove the seeds from the okra and cut into thin rings.

❷ Heat the olive oil in a large saucepan and fry the shallots. Add the garlic and fry briefly. Next add the okra and aubergine (eggplant), cover and cook for about 8 minutes.

❸ Add the vegetable stock (broth). Season with thyme, allspice, chilli and lime juice and simmer the vegetables for another 5 minutes.

❹ Put the spinach in the pan and let it soften. Add the coconut milk and milk. Bring to the boil again and season the vegetable stew with salt and pepper. Sprinkle with the chopped coriander leaves and serve.

Serves 2. About 100 kcal per serving

Asparagus gratin

The Gorgonzola adds a subtle touch to this dish. The Gorgonzola can be replaced with other blue cheeses, such as Roquefort which is milder but saltier than Gorgonzola.

2 kg/4 1/2 lb white asparagus

salt

1 pinch sugar

butter

3 tomatoes

2 onion

2–3 tablespoons finely chopped basil

freshly ground pepper

150 g/5 1/2 oz Gorgonzola

3 tablespoons crème fraîche

❶ Peel the asparagus, remove the woody ends. Cook the asparagus in salted water with a pinch of sugar and a little butter for 10 minutes until done. Remove the asparagus from the water, drain and put in a well buttered gratin dish.

❷ Blanch the tomatoes, skin and chop up. Peel the onion, chop finely and braise lightly in the hot butter together with the chopped tomatoes. Add the basil, season with salt and pepper and pour the sauce over the asparagus.

❸ Cut the cheese into small cubes, stir into the crème fraîche and pour over the tomatoes and asparagus. Brown under the pre-heated oven grill for about 5 minutes.

Serves 4. About 302 kcal per serving

Wok-fried vegetables

When eating food prepared in a wok, you can eat to your heart's content because the vegetables contain no fat and only one tablespoon of oil is used to fry all the vegetables. The vegetables are only fried for a short time so they remain crisp and do not lose their vitamins and minerals.

1 Wash and prepare the pepper and cut into thin strips. Peel the celeriac and carrots and cut into thin sticks. Wash and prepare the spring onions (scallions) and cut into rings. Wash the bean sprouts and drain.

2 Peel the ginger and garlic and chop finely. Heat the groundnut oil in the wok and briefly fry the ginger and garlic but do not allow to go brown. Add the vegetables and mushrooms and fry for about 3–5 minutes, stirring continuously. The vegetables should remain crisp.

3 Stir together the vegetable stock (broth), soy sauce and cornflour (corn starch). Pour over the vegetables and bring briefly to the boil. Season with chilli, lemon juice and pepper.

Serves 2. About 170 kcal per serving

1 red sweet pepper

1/2 celeriac root

1 carrot

100 g/3 1/2 oz mushrooms

2 spring onions (scallions)

100 g/3 1/2 oz fresh soy sauce

1 small piece fresh root ginger

1 clove garlic

1 tablespoon groundnut oil

200 ml/7 fl oz (7/8 cup) vegetable stock (broth)

3 tablespoons soy sauce

1 teaspoon cornflour (corn starch)

1 pinch chilli pepper

1 teaspoon lemon juice

freshly ground pepper

Aubergine and courgette (eggplant and zucchini) rolls with tomato sauce

For this sophisticated recipe a slicing machine makes it easier to cut the aubergines (eggplants) and courgettes (zucchini) into very regular, thin slices. Delicious with hot ciabatta bread and a glass of Italian red wine.

1 Slice the aubergines (eggplants) and courgettes (zucchini) lengthways into very thin slices.

2 Heat 1 tablespoon of oil in a pan, add the breadcrumbs and fry until golden brown, stirring continuously. Then add the parsley, basil, Parmesan and one of the garlic cloves, stirring well.

3 Spread a layer of the herb mixture on the aubergine (eggplant) and courgette (zucchini) slices, roll them up in slices of mozzarella and secure with cocktail sticks.

4 Heat 1 tablespoon olive oil in a pan, add the courgette (zucchini) and aubergine (eggplant) rolls and fry for 10 minutes; keep in a warm place.

5 For the tomato sauce: peel the onion and cloves of garlic and chop finely. Heat 1 tablespoon of olive oil in a saucepan, add the onion and garlic and sweat until transparent. Drain the tomatoes, crush with a fork and add to the onion and garlic. Pour in the red wine. Bring to the boil and simmer until cooked. Season with salt, pepper and chilli powder.

6 Put the aubergine (eggplant) and courgette (zucchini) rolls in the tomato sauce, cover and allow to stand for about 10 minutes. Arrange the rolls on four plates with the tomato sauce.

Serves 4. About 388 kcal per serving

2 aubergines (eggplants)

2 courgettes (zucchini)

200 g/7 oz mozzarella

4 tablespoons olive oil

3 tablespoons breadcrumbs

1 bunch parsley, finely chopped

1 bunch basil, finely chopped

2 cloves garlic, finely chopped

40 g/1 1/2 oz (3/8 cup) freshly grated Parmesan

salt

freshly ground pepper

1 onion

1 can chopped tomatoes (800 g/1 3/4 lb)

4 tablespoons red wine

chilli powder

Spinach omelette

Tortilla is one of the most popular kind of tapas. Originally made with potatoes, it is now served as various combinations with vegetables, cheese or ham. A tortilla may be served warm or cold.

1 Wash spinach, remove stems and chop coarsely. Peel potatoes and slice thinly. Heat 4 tablepoons of olive oil in a pan and fry potatoes for about 15 minutes until done. Remove from pan and keep warm.

2 Peel onion and chop finely, seed chilli and chop finely, too. Pour 2 tablespoons of olive oil in a pan and fry onions and chili. Add spinach, sauté for 3 minutes and remove from pan.

3 Beat eggs with salt and pepper, heat remaining oil in pan and leave eggs to thicken briefly, spread mixture of potatoes and spinach over it.

4 Bake tortilla at low heat for about 10 minutes in a pan. Slide it carefully onto a serving dish and divide like a cake. Wash chives and chop finely. Garnish tortilla with rolls of chives.

Serves 4. About 370 kcal per serving

200 g fresh spinach

3 potatoes

8 tablespoons olive oil

1 onion

1 red chilli

5 eggs

salt

freshly ground black pepper

1 bunch chives

Tomatoes stuffed with onions

The onion is the most versatile of vegetables. This dish combining onions, tomatoes, garlic, capers and olives will add a festive note to any table.

1 Peel the onions and chop finely. Heat the oil in a pan. Add the onions and fry. Add the porridge (rolled) oats and stir well. Put the onion mixture in a warm place.

2 Peel the cloves of garlic and chop up with the capers and olives. Add to the onion mixture and season with oregano, salt and pepper.

3 Pre-heat the oven to 220°C (425°F), Gas mark 7. Butter a large gratin dish generously.

4 Cut the tops off the tomatoes and carefully scoop out the pulp using a teaspoon. Sprinkle the scooped out tomatoes lightly with salt and leave them to stand for about 10 minutes. Stuff the tomatoes with a generous amount of the onion mixture, which can be higher than the edges of the scooped out tomatoes. Replace the lids. Put the stuffed tomatoes next to each other in the gratin dish and bake on the middle shelf of the oven for about 30 minutes.

Serves 4. About 269 kcal per serving

300 g/11 oz onions

5 tablespoons oil

70 g/3 oz (1 cup) porridge (rolled) oats

2 cloves garlic

20 g/3⁄4 oz capers

50 g/2 oz green olives stuffed with pimento

oregano

salt

pepper

butter for the mould

800 g/1 3⁄4 lb medium tomatoes

Red pepper traybakes

In Catalonia, you get these traybakes with a vast selection of fish, meat, vegetables and poultry. Here is a wonderful example of a vegetable pie.

❶ Dissolve yeast in 50 ml of lukewarm water, mix with a sprinkling of sugar and 1 tablespoon of flour, set aside and leave to rise.

❷ Knead half of butter with egg. Spread flour on table-top, make a slight hollow in centre, place dough in it and gradually add butter with egg and warmed orange juice. Knead until a smooth (not too dry) dough is obtained. Set aside and leave to rise.

❸ Cook peppers in a well preheated oven at 200 °C (400 °F) for about 30 minutes, skin, seed and cut into strips. Peel garlic cloves, slice, fold into peppers and season with salt and pepper.

❹ Grease rectangular baking tray with remaining butter, roll dough and place on tray. Spread peppers and garlic over dough and bake in hot oven at 220 °C (450 °F) for about 30 minutes.

❺ Spread black olives over tray 5 minutes before baking time is over, remove tray from oven and sprinkle with olive oil. May be served warm or cold.

Serves 4. About 1020 kcal per serving

20 g yeast

sprinkling sugar

500 g flour

100 g butter

1 egg

100 ml orange juice

4 large red peppers

2 cloves of garlic

salt

freshly ground pepper

100 g black olives

100 ml olive oil

Potato gnocchi with Shiitake mushrooms

Shiitake mushrooms are native to the Far East where they are cultivated on the trunks of oak trees and Shii trees. They have been a much appreciated vegetable in China for centuries. Fresh Shiitake mushrooms are available in shops specialising in oriental food.

❶ Peel the potatoes, cut into dice and cook in boiling water for about 15 minutes until soft. Drain, push through a potato press or mash, then leave to cool down. Season with salt, add the flour and work into a dough. Leave to rest for 15 minutes.

❷ Meanwhile peel the onions and chop finely. Clean the mushrooms, wipe with kitchen paper and cut into thin slices. Drain the tomatoes and reserve the oil. Cut the tomatoes into thin strips.

❸ Sprinkle flour on the worktop and roll out the dough to make a cylinder about 2.5 cm/1 in in diameter. Cut into pieces about 5 cm/2 in long and make a grooved pattern in them with a fork. Bring a large amount of salted water to the boil, add the gnocchi and cook. They are ready when they rise to the surface.

❹ In the meantime, heat the tomato oil in a second pan and fry the onion until golden yellow. Add the mushrooms, fry briefly and take out of the pan. Add the port and mushroom stock (broth) to the cooking fat and reduce to one-third. Season with herb salt and pepper. Add the butter gradually in small amounts and work into the sauce with a wooden spoon. Add the mushrooms and heat them in the port-flavoured butter.

❺ Drain the gnocchi using a skimming ladle and add the strips of sun-dried tomatoes. Arrange the gnocchi with the mushroom and port wine sauce on two warmed plates and sprinkle with parsley.

Serves 2. About 450 kcal per serving

400 g/14 oz floury potatoes

sea salt

about 75 g/3 oz (3⁄4 cup) flour

1 small onion

150 g/5 oz Shiitake mushrooms

2 sun-dried tomatoes preserved in oil

75 ml/3 fl oz (3⁄8 cup) white port

100 ml/31⁄2 fl oz (1⁄2 cup) mushroom stock (broth) (from the carton)

herb salt

freshly ground pepper

1 tablespoon butter

1 tablespoon chopped parsley

flour for the work surface

Pizza Margherita

This famous pizza was created in honour of Queen Margherita of Italy, and it displays the three colours of the Italian flag: green basil, white mozzarella and red tomatoes.

20 g/3⁄4 oz yeast

300 g/11 oz flour

1 pinch salt

olive oil for the baking sheet

2 tablespoons olive oil

flour for the work surface

for the topping:

500 g/18 oz fresh tomatoes

250 g/9 oz mozzarella

1 small bunch basil

salt

ground white pepper

6 tablespoons olive oil

❶ To make the dough: crumble the yeast which should be at room temperature in a cup, add 2 tablespoons lukewarm water and stir. Sift the flour into a large bowl, add salt and make a well in the centre. Pour in the yeast mixture and sprinkle a little flour on top. Put in a warm place to rise until it has doubled in size.

❷ Add 125 ml/4 fl oz (1/2 cup) of lukewarm water to the risen dough and work vigorously by hand or with the dough hook of the mixer. Knead vigorously until the dough becomes smooth with an elastic consistency. Shape into a ball, cover and put in a warm place to rise until it has doubled in height.

❸ Pre-heat the oven to 220°C (425°F), Gas mark 7. Grease a baking sheet with olive oil. On it, knead the dough again vigorously but briefly to work in the olive oil. Roll out flat on a lightly floured work surface and form a slightly raised edge.

❹ For the topping: peel the tomatoes, cut them into quarters and remove the seeds. Cut the tomato quarters into strips and arrange on the pizza base. Now add the thinly sliced mozzarella and basil leaves. Season with salt and pepper and sprinkle with olive oil. Bake the pizza on the bottom shelf of the oven for about 30 minutes.

Serves 4. About 574 kcal per serving

fat for the baking sheet

10 g (2 teaspoons) fresh yeast or
   5 g (1 teaspoon) dried yeast

250 g/9 oz (2 1/4 cups) flour

75 g/3 oz (6 tablespoons) melted
   butter

salt

500 g/18 oz medium tomatoes

500 g/18 oz courgettes (zucchini)

flour for the work surface

100 g/3 1/2 oz (1 cup) grated
   Gruyère cheese,

100 ml/3 1/2 oz (scant 1/2 cup)
   sour cream

2 eggs

1 tablespoon dried herbs of
   Provence

Tomato flan with courgettes (zucchini)

What distinguishes the tomato quiche from a pizza is the sour cream with beaten eggs and herbs which is poured over the vegetables. So as an alternative you can make a delicious pizza by coating the base with tomato sauce, arranging the vegetables on it and sprinkling the top with oregano, grated cheese and a little olive oil.

1 Pre-heat the oven to 220°C (425°F), Gas mark 7. Grease a baking-tin.

2 Crumble the yeast into 150 ml/4 fl oz (5⁄8 cup) lukewarm water and stir well. Sift the flour over a bowl and add the yeast with the water, melted butter and a pinch of salt. Stir to make a smooth mixture. Cover the bowl with a tea towel. Leave to rise in a warm place for about 15 minutes.

3 Halve the tomatoes, remove the seeds and slice. Clean and wash the courgettes (zucchini) and slice.

4 Roll out the yeast dough on a floured work surface and transfer to the baking tin. Press the dough down, pull into shape and form an edge. Prick the base with a fork.

5 Arrange the tomato and courgette (zucchini) slices on the base. Season with salt and sprinkle with grated cheese.

6 Stir the sour cream until smooth and add the beaten eggs and herbs. Stir again. Pour this mixture over the vegetables. Put on the bottom shelf of the oven and bake for 30–40 minutes. Serve hot.

Serves 4. About 649 kcal per serving

Asparagus gratin on a bed of spinach

The white asparagus and green spinach, topped with Gruyère, is both a delightful visual combination and a tasty, nourishing dish.

❶ Peel the asparagus, remove the woody ends and cook the asparagus in boiling salted water with a pinch of sugar and 10 g/⅜ oz (2 teaspoons) butter for 10 minutes until done.

❷ Wash the spinach, blanch in boiling salted water, remove, drain and press a little to squeeze out any remaining water. Butter an ovenproof dish, put half the spinach on top and cover with the asparagus.

❸ Cut the remaining spinach into strips and put on top of the asparagus, dot some flakes of butter on top and cover with the slices of Gruyère. Bake on the lowest shelf of the oven pre-heated to 220°C/425°F (gas 7). After about 15 minutes, put under the grill for a further 3 minutes until golden brown.

Serves 4. About 670 kcal per serving

2 kg/4 1/2 lb white asparagus

salt

1 pinch sugar

90 g/3 oz (6 tablespoons) butter

800 g/1 3⁄4 lb leaf spinach

450 g/1 lb Gruyère, sliced

Tomatoes à la Provençale

These baked tomatoes seasoned with herbs of Provence conjure up images of sun, sea, sand… and France.

❶ Pre-heat the oven to 220°C (425°F), Gas mark 7. Butter a baking tin generously. Peel the garlic.

❷ Add the herbs and pressed garlic to the oil. Season with salt and pepper.

❸ Cut the tomatoes into three, remove the seeds and salt lightly. Place the tomato pieces in the baking tin and pour the herb oil over them.

❹ Put on the middle shelf of the oven and bake for 30 minutes.

Serves 4. About 221 kcal per serving

butter for the mould

2 cloves garlic

8 tablespoons olive oil

2 tablespoons dried herbs of Provence

salt

white pepper from the mill

8 medium tomatoes

500 g/18 oz green asparagus

salt

1 pinch sugar

45 g/1 1/2 oz (3 tablespoons) butter

45 g/1 1/2 oz (1/2 cup) flour

250 ml/8 fl oz (1 cup) milk

1 teaspoon vegetable stock (broth)

freshly grated nutmeg

freshly ground pepper

3 eggs

6 tablespoons parsley

100 g/3 1/2 oz (1 cup) grated Emmenthal

fat for the mould

Asparagus soufflé

A soufflé is much easier to make than many people believe. However, it is most important that all the ingredients should be prepared very quickly and that the soufflé should be served as soon as it is ready. It is vital that the oven door should not be opened during the first half hour; if it is, the soufflé will collapse.

1 Wash the asparagus, remove the woody ends and put 4 asparagus stalks (stems) to one side. Cut the rest of the asparagus into pieces 1 cm/3/4 in long. Simmer the asparagus pieces gently in salted water with sugar for 10 minutes until done. Remove from the water, drain and separate the tips from the rest of the asparagus pieces.

2 Melt the butter, stir in the flour and brown lightly. Add the milk, stirring constantly and allow to thicken. Stir in the vegetable stock (broth). Season with salt, nutmeg and pepper. Allow the sauce to cool down a little.

3 Separate the eggs. Stir in the finely chopped parsley, grated cheese and egg yolk. Slice the raw asparagus very finely and stir into the sauce. Add a pinch of salt to the egg whites, beat vigorously to form stiff peaks. Fold gently into the sauce.

4 Put the asparagus pieces in a well-greased gratin dish. Pour in the soufflé mixture and bake on the middle shelf for 25–30 minutes in the oven pre-heated to 220°C (425°F), Gas mark 7.

4 Remove the soufflé from the oven. Garnish with the asparagus tips.

Serves 4. About 325 kcal per serving

Chinese fried vegetables with smoked tofu

A light, easy to digest vegetarian dish for brain-workers, rich in minerals, trace elements and vitamins which strengthen the immune system. It can be prepared in 20 minutes and made with a wide range of vegetables and pasta.

❶ Bring plenty of boiling water to the boil, add the buckwheat pasta and cook following the instructions on the packet. Peel the carrots, shallots and garlic. Cut the carrots into small cubes. Chop the onion and garlic finely. Clean the mushrooms and dice small. Rinse the bean sprouts and drain the pasta.

❷ Heat the sesame oil in a deep pan or wok and fry the shallots, garlic, carrots, mushrooms and bean sprouts for 5 minutes, stirring continuously. Cut the smoked tofu into cubes and add to the frying vegetables.

❸ Fry briefly but briskly and season with soy sauce, lime juice, salt and pepper. Sprinkle with chopped coriander just before serving

Serves 2. About 305 kcal per serving

sea salt

100 g/3 1⁄2 oz buckwheat pasta

3 large carrots

2 shallots

1 clove garlic

120 g/4 oz oyster mushrooms

50 g/2 oz soy sauce

2 teaspoons sesame oil

100 g/3 1⁄2 oz smoked tofu

soy sauce

1 teaspoon lime juice

freshly ground pepper

1 tablespoon chopped green coriander

Tortillas stuffed with peppers and sweet corn

1 small sweet pepper

1 small onion

1 teaspoon olive oil

100 g/3 1/2 oz sweetcorn (from
the can)

salt

cayenne pepper

some dried thyme

2 tortillas

A Mexican snack which does not require much preparation. Tortillas can be bought ready-made in the supermarket and the vegetables are fried only very briefly.

1 Clean the pepper, remove the stalk and seeds and cut into fine strips. Peel the onion and chop finely. Heat the olive oil in a non-stick pan and fry the pepper for about 5 minutes.

2 Drain the sweet corn, add to the pan and heat up briefly. Season the vegetables with salt, cayenne pepper and thyme.

3 Heat the tortillas in the oven for a few minutes following the instructions on the packet and remove from the oven. Place the vegetables on the hot tortillas and roll them up.

Serves 2. About 185 kcal per serving

Asparagus flan

Béchamel sauce is a component of many classic asparagus dishes because it enhances the delicate flavour of asparagus.

500 g/18 oz asparagus, mixed

salt

10 g/3⁄8 oz (2 teaspoons) butter

1 teaspoon sugar

500 ml/17 fl oz (2 1/4 cups) béchamel sauce (ready-made product)

100 g/3 1/2 oz curd cheese

yolks of 2 eggs

100 g/3 1/2 oz celeriac

2–3 teaspoons dill

freshly ground white pepper

300 g/11 oz puff pastry, frozen

flour for the work surface

❶ Peel the asparagus, remove the woody ends and cut the asparagus stalks (stems) into pieces 2 cm/3⁄4 in long. Heat water in a large saucepan. As soon as the water boils, add the salt, butter and sugar. Add the asparagus and cook for about 10 minutes until done. Pour away the water and drain well.

❷ Mix the béchamel sauce, curd cheese and egg yolk in a bowl and stir until the mixture is creamy. Grate the cheese and add to the béchamel sauce together with the chopped dill. Stir well and season with white pepper.

❸ Rinse the flan tin in cold water and drain. Place the defrosted puff pastry on a floured work surface and roll out to the size of the flan tin. Line the flan tin with the dough and press the dough into along the edges. If necessary, cut off the excess dough with a flat knife. Pour the béchamel sauce into the flan tin and add the asparagus pieces, making sure that they are all covered by the sauce.

❹ Bake for about 20 minutes in the oven pre-heated to 200°C (400°F), Gas mark 6.

Serves 4. About 997 kcal per serving

1 medium courgette (zucchini)

3 large carrots

1 tablespoon lemon juice

freshly ground pepper

1/2 bunch parsley

1 egg

1 tablespoon oat flakes

1 tablespoon sunflower oil

125 g/4 1/2 oz low-fat quark

1 tablespoon low-fat milk (1.5%)

1 bunch chives

1/2 small box cress

Vegetable pancakes (crepes) with herb quark

A light dish which can be prepared with a variety of vegetables. In this recipe, carrots and courgettes (zucchini) are coarsely grated and fried until crisp in a non-stick pan with very little fat. It is delicious served with a home-made herb quark dip.

❶ Wash and prepare the courgette (zucchini), peel the carrots and grate both coarsely. Season with salt and pepper.

❷ Wash the parsley, pat dry, chop the leaves finely and add to the vegetables. Next add the egg and oats and stir well into the vegetables.

❸ Heat the sunflower oil in a non-stick pan. Using a tablespoon, take small portions of the vegetable mixture, put in the pan, press flat and fry on both sides until crisp. Repeat the operation until all the mixture has been used up.

❹ Put the low-fat quark and milk in a small bowl, stir until smooth and season with pepper. Wash and chop the chives and cress, then add to the quark. Arrange the vegetable pancakes with the herb quark on two plates.

Serves 2. About 190 kcal per serving

Grilled avocados with tomato and bread stuffing

As well as being delicious served cold in salad or in a guacamole dip for spicy crisps, avocados are also excellent in hot dishes such as this vegetable gratin with tomatoes. Their flavour combines beautifully with the sweet-and-sour taste of the tomatoes.

1 Drain the tomato pieces, peel the shallots and cut into thin rings. Remove the crusts from the coriander bread and cut into 1 cm/⅜ in cubes. Chop up the basil.

2 Heat 2 tablespoons of oil in a pan, add the bread cubes and fry on all sides. Pour the bread cubes with the fat into a large bowl. Add the tomato pieces, onion rings and basil and stir well. Season with salt, pepper and vinegar.

3 Pre-heat the oven to 220°C (425°F), Gas mark 7.

4 Cut the avocados in half lengthways, remove the stone (seed) and scoop out some of the flesh with a tablespoon. Dice the scooped-out flesh and immediately sprinkle it and the avocado halves with lemon juice. Add the diced avocado flesh to the bread mixture and stir it in.

5 Fill the avocado halves with the bread mixture. Mix the breadcrumbs and Parmesan with the rest of the oil and pour over the stuffing.

6 Put the avocados next to each other in a gratin dish. Cook on the middle shelf of the oven for about 20 minutes until brown.

Serves 4. About 446 kcal per serving

1 can chopped tomatoes
(400 g/14 oz)

4 shallots

2 slices coriander bread

1 bunch of basil

5 tablespoons vegetable oil

salt

white pepper

1 teaspoon balsamic vinegar

2 avocados

juice of 1 lemon

2 tablespoons breadcrumbs

1 tablespoon grated Parmesan

Green asparagus with lemon marinade

This light, easy-to-make dish is an ideal starter. While the asparagus is marinating, the rest of the meal can be prepared.

❶ Wash the asparagus. and remove the ends. Blanch the asparagus in boiling salted water with sugar and butter. Remove from the water, drain and arrange in a shallow dish.

❷ Wash the lemon in hot water, wipe dry and thinly grate the zest of half the lemon. Squeeze out the juice. Season the 3–4 tablespoons of lemon juice with salt and pepper and add the oil to make a marinade. Wash the chives, dry, chop finely and add to the marinade.

❸ Sprinkle the marinade and lemon zest over the asparagus and leave to stand for 2 hours. Garnish with lemon balm before serving

Serves 4. About 171 kcal per serving

1 kg/2 1/4 lb green asparagus

salt

1/2 teaspoon sugar

1 teaspoon butter

juice and zest of 1 untreated lemon

freshly ground pepper

4 tablespoons sunflower oil

1 bunch chives

lemon balm as garnish

Asparagus gratin with Parmesan

A gratin need not always mean potatoes! An asparagus gratin requires very few ingredients, takes very little time to prepare and is perfect as a starter or side dish.

❶ Wash the green asparagus, peel the white asparagus and remove the woody ends. Cook the asparagus in salted water with a pinch of sugar for about 10 minutes until done. Remove from the water and drain.

❷ Put the asparagus in a greased gratin dish, sprinkle with Parmesan and dot with flakes of herb butter. Brown under the preheated grill for 3 minutes.

Serves 4. About 392 kcal per serving

500 g/18 oz green asparagus

500 g/18 oz white asparagus

salt

1 pinch sugar

200 g/7 oz grated Parmesan

125 g/4 1/2 oz (5/8 cup) herb butter

Fried grated potatoes with apples

The humble fried potato can become interesting if combined with the right ingredients. This caramelised apple is an exotic variation for those who like to experiment.

1 Wash the apples thoroughly, remove the cores and quarter. Dice small.

2 Melt the butter over a medium heat. Add the diced apple and stir into the butter. Add lemon juice, sugar and cinnamon and simmer over a low heat, stirring continuously until the apples are soft and golden brown. Remove from the pan and put in a bowl.

3 Peel the onion and chop finely. Wash and peel the potatoes, grate them with a cheese grater, put them in a clean tea towel and press out the liquid. Put the onions in a bowl with the potatoes and season with salt and pepper.

4 Heat oil in a large frying pan. Carefully drop in spoonfuls of the potato and onion mixture, press flat and fry for about 6 minutes, turning occasionally. Remove from the pan and drain on kitchen paper.

5 Wash parsley and chop fine.

6 Place a tablespoonful of the caramelised apple mixture on each potato cake. Garnish with sour cream and parsley.

Serves four, 250 kcal per serving

250 g/8 oz untreated eating apples
4 tablespoons butter
1 teaspoon lemon juice
1 teaspoon sugar
1 shake of cinnamon
1/2 onion
2 floury potatoes
salt
freshly ground black pepper
oil
1/2 bunch parsley for garnishing
50 ml/2 fl oz (1/4 cup) sour cream

Tomato and couscous bake

250 g/9 oz couscous

butter for the mould

4 large beef tomatoes

2 tablespoons oil

1 tablespoon parsley, chopped

1 bay leaf

salt

pepper

100 g/3 1/2 oz (1 cup) grated Emmenthal cheese

Couscous dishes are very popular in North African countries such as Tunisia. It may also be served as a salad with fresh vegetables.

❶ Put the couscous in a bowl and pour a little hot water over it – the couscous must be moist but not sitting in water. Cover the bowl with a large lid or aluminium foil and leave to soak for a few minutes.

❷ Pre-heat the oven to 220°C (425°F), Gas mark 7. Butter a soufflé dish generously.

❸ Cut the tomatoes into quarters, remove the seeds and chop coarsely. Heat the oil in a large pan and add the chopped tomatoes, parsley and bay leaves; season generously with salt and pepper. Cover and simmer over a low heat for about 30 minutes until the mixture has reduced to make a thick sauce. Stir now and again.

❹ Put a layer of couscous at the bottom of the soufflé dish with a layer of tomato purée on top. Follow with a layer of grated cheese, another layer of couscous and finally a layer of tomato purée. Sprinkle with grated cheese. Bake the soufflé for about 20 minutes in the oven.

Serves 4. About 179 kcal per serving

Tomato omelette with basil and goat's cheese

A small snack for four people, but with ciabatta or French bread and a mixed salad, it makes a delicious light meal for two. A garnish of black olives completes this nourishing meal.

1 Peel and quarter the tomatoes; remove the seeds. Cut the tomato quarters into cubes. Melt 15 g/1/2 oz (1 tablespoon) butter in a saucepan, add the diced tomatoes and cook gently for 5 minutes. Leave to cool.

2 Beat the eggs with herb salt and pepper in a bowl; stir in the tomatoes.

3 Melt the remaining butter in a pan and make two omelettes from the egg and tomato mixture.

4 Cut the omelettes in half and put on a warm plate. Garnish with basil and sprinkle the goat's cheese on top.

Serves 4. About 208 kcal per serving

3 firm tomatoes

30 g/1 oz (2 tablespoons) butter

5 eggs

herb salt

freshly ground pepper

6 leaves fresh basil

80 g/3 oz goat's cheese, crumbled

Apple and onion quiche

This dish makes a delicious snack, or a light supper served with a fresh salad. Individual quiches can be reheated next day as needed.

1 Grate 75 g/3 oz (3/4 cup) of the cheese. Sift the flour into a bowl with a pinch of salt and 1/4 teaspoon of mustard powder. Add the margarine and the grated cheese. Mix with 2 tablespoons of water and knead the ingredients together to a smooth dough. Refrigerate.

2 For the filling: Peel the onions and chop small. Peel, quarter and core the apples. Grate the quarters finely. Heat 25 g/1 oz (2 tablespoons) of the butter in a saucepan and sauté the onions until transparent. Stir in the grated apples and cook for another 2 to 3 minutes. Remove the pan from the heat and let the apple mixture cool.

3 Pre-heat oven to 200°C (400°F), Gas Mark 6.

4 Grease a spring-form mould with the remaining butter. Take the dough out of the refrigerator, roll out with a rolling pin and line the spring-form mould. Leave in a cool place for 20 minutes, then bake in the pre-heated oven for 20 minutes.

5 Wash the parsley and chop finely. Break the eggs into a bowl, add the double (heavy) cream, herbs, parsley, salt, the remaining mustard powder and some pepper and beat with a whisk until foaming. Grate 60 g/2 oz (1/2 cup) of the cheese and stir into the egg mixture. Cut the rest of the cheese into slices. Put the apple and onion mixture in the pre-baked pie case and pour the egg mixture over it. Arrange the cheese slices on top.

6 Reduce the oven temperature to 190°C (375°F), Gas Mark 5, and bake the quiche for about 20 minutes until it is a beautiful golden colour.

Serves 4. About 850 kcal per serving

190 g/7 oz Gruyère cheese

225 g/8 oz (2 1/4 cups) plain (all purpose) flour

salt

3/4 teaspoon mustard powder

75 g/3 oz (6 tablepsoons) margarine

1 onion

400 g/14 oz eating apples

40 g/1 1/2 oz (3 tablespoons) butter

2 to 3 eggs

150 ml/5 fl oz (5/8 cup) double (heavy) cream

1 teaspoon dried mixed herbs

1/2 bunch parsley

freshly ground black pepper

Tomato and goat's cheese bread gratin

This simple little dish can also be prepared with mild sheep's milk cheese. Instead of walnuts and basil, you can sprinkle the gratin with pine nuts and thyme or oregano, fresh or dried.

5 large tomatoes

200 g/7 oz goat's cheese

herb salt

freshly ground pepper

1/2 baguette

7 tablespoons olive oil

35 g/1 1/2 oz (3/8 cup) coarsely chopped walnut kernels

1 small bunch basil, finely chopped

❶ Slice the tomatoes and goat's cheese. Sprinkle herb salt and a little freshly ground pepper on the tomato slices. Cut the baguette diagonally into 12 slices.

❷ Pre-heat the oven to 200°C (400°F), Gas mark 6. Heat 4 tablespoons of olive oil in a pan. Fry the baguette slices briefly on both sides and leave to cool slightly.

❸ Grease a gratin dish with 1 tablespoon of oil. Arrange the slices of bread, tomatoes and cheese in alternate layers in the gratin dish. Pour the rest of the olive oil over the gratin. Bake in the oven for about 10 minutes.

❹ Shortly before the gratin is ready to come out of the oven, sprinkle with walnuts and basil. Serve hot.

Serves 4. About 433 kcal per serving

Mashed potato gratin with tomato sauce

This mashed potato gratin served with tomato sauce is a delicious, light vegetarian dish which your children will definitely like very much.

1 Boil unpeeled potatoes for about 25 minutes until soft. Pre-heat the oven to 220°C (425°F), Gas mark 7.

2 Peel the boiled potatoes, put in a bowl and mash with a fork. Add the Parmesan, butter, milk and egg. Purée this mixture in a blender until it is smooth and homogenous. If it seems too dry, add some milk. Season the mash with salt, pepper and nutmeg.

3 Put the mashed potato in four small moulds and cook on the middle shelf of the oven for 15 –20 minutes until golden brown.

4 For the tomato sauce: cut the tomatoes into four and dice finely. Peel the shallots and cloves of garlic, chop finely.

5 Heat the oil in a saucepan, add the chopped garlic and shallots and fry. Add the diced tomatoes and tomato ketchup; season with herbs, a little sugar, salt and pepper. Simmer the tomato sauce for about 10 minutes. Remove the rosemary.

6 Serve the tomato sauce hot with the mashed potato gratin.

Serves 4. About 379 kcal per serving

1 kg/2 1/4 lb potatoes, cooked floury

1 tablespoon grated Parmesan

60 g/2 oz (4 tablespoons) butter

250 ml/8 fl oz (1 cup) milk

1 egg

nutmeg

pepper

salt

600 g/11/4 lb ripe tomatoes

2 shallots

1 clove garlic

oil for the pan

1 teaspoon tomato ketchup

1/2 teaspoon dried Italian herbs

1 small sprig rosemary

sugar

Pasta & rice dishes

sea salt

300 g/10 oz tagliatelle

300 g/10 oz fresh leaf spinach

2 shallots

2 cloves garlic

1 tablespoon pine kernels

2 teaspoons olive oil

100 ml/3 1/2 fl oz (1/2 cup) low-
   fat milk (1.5%)

1 teaspoon sauce thickening

herb salt

freshly ground pepper

frisch grated nutmeg

30 g/1 oz (1 cup) grated Pecorino
   cheese

Tagliatelle with spinach

A delicious dish which is quick and easy to prepare! It can be served as a main course with a root vegetable salad, but also as a starter.

1 Bring a large saucepan of salted water to the boil and cook the tagliatelle "al dente" following the instructions on the packet. Remove any damaged leaves and coarse stalks and wash the spinach. Peel the shallots and garlic and chop finely. Fry the pine kernels until golden yellow.

2 Heat the olive oil in a pan and fry the shallots until golden brown, add the garlic and fry briefly. Add the spinach, let it collapse, cover and cook gently over a low flame for about 3 minutes. Add the milk, bring to the boil and stir in the sauce thickening. Cook until the sauce has thickened, stirring all the time. Season the spinach with herb salt, pepper and a touch of nutmeg.

3 Drain the tagliatelle and arrange with the spinach on two warmed plates. Sprinkle with the fried pine kernels and Pecorino cheese.

Serves 2. About 745 kcal per serving

Sage pasta with artichokes and courgettes (zucchini)

A versatile light vegetable dish. It can be served as a main meal with a crisp salad, or as the "pasta" course in an Italian-style menu.

❶ Peel the shallots and garlic and chop finely. Wash the artichokes and remove the stems, basal leaves and hard leaf ends. Cut the artichokes into four. Wash and prepare the courgettes (zucchini) and cut into sticks.

❷ Heat the oil in a saucepan. Fry the shallots, then add the garlic and fry briefly. Add the vegetable stock (broth), wine and artichokes. Cover and cook over a low heat for about 25 minutes. Add the courgette (zucchini) pieces and simmer for a further 5 minutes. Add the crème fraîche and season with salt and pepper.

❸ Cook the pasta in salted boiling water until it is "al dente", following the instructions on the packet. Drain. Cut the sage leaves into strips and stir into the pasta. Arrange the pasta with the vegetables on two warmed plates. Sprinkle with Parmesan.

Serves 2. About 365 kcal per serving.

1 shallot

1 clove garlic

4 baby artichokes

200 g/7 oz small courgettes (zucchini)

1 teaspoon olive oil

150 ml/5 fl oz (5⁄8 cup) vegetable stock (broth)

2 tablespoons dry white wine

1 tablespoon crème fraîche

sea salt

freshly ground pepper

125 g/4 1⁄2 oz pasta (e.g. tagliatelle)

4 small leaves sage

freshly grated Parmesan

Spaghetti with tomato sauce

This classic Italian dish is always popular and can be endlessly varied. This sauce is made from fresh tomatoes and red pepper, giving it a distinctive sweetish spicy taste. It can be prepared the day before.

1 clove garlic

1 leek

1 tablespoon olive oil

300 g/10 oz fresh tomatoes

1 red sweet pepper

1/2 small chilli pepper

200 ml/7 fl oz (7/8 cup) vegetable stock (broth)

salt

250 g/9 oz spaghetti

cayenne pepper

1/2 teaspoon sugar

1 tablespoon fresh oregano leaves

❶ Peel the garlic and crush. Wash and prepare the leek and cut into thin rounds. Heat the olive oil in a shallow casserole and briefly fry the garlic and leek in it.

❷ Wash the tomatoes, remove the stalk and cut into eight pieces. Wash the pepper, remove the stalk and seeds and cut into thin strips. Add both to the casserole and fry. Wash the chilli, cut lengthways, remove the seeds and chop finely. Add the chilli and vegetable stock (broth) to the pan. Cover and braise for about 15 minutes.

❸ Bring the salted water to the boil in a large saucepan and cook the pasta "al dente" following the instructions on the packet.

❹ Season the tomato and pepper sauce with cayenne pepper, salt and a little sugar. Wash the oregano leaves, dab dry and chop the leaves finely. Boil down to thicken a little more.

❺ Put the spaghetti in two bowls and pour the sauce on top.

Serves 2. About 550 kcal per serving

1.5 kg/3 lb white asparagus

salt

1 pinch sugar

10 g/3⁄8 oz (2 teaspoons) butter

600 g/1 1⁄4 lb fresh ravioli with ricotta filling

1 shallot

6 tablespoons white wine-vine-gar

freshly ground pepper

4 tablespoons broth

yolks of 2 eggs

2 tablespoons olive oil

2 tablespoons tarragon, finely chopped

3 tablespoons chopped tomatoes

cayenne pepper

Asparagus ravioli

Ravioli with ricotta filling are available from supermarkets and Italian delicatessen. They can be either frozen or fresh.

❶ Peel the asparagus and remove the woody ends. Cook in boiling salted water with sugar and butter until done.

❷ Cook the ravioli "al dente" in gently simmering water.

❸ Peel the shallots, dice and cook with the vinegar and pepper. Reduce to thicken the mixture. Add the stock (broth).

❹ Add 2 tablespoons water to the egg yolk and beat in a bain-marie until it becomes creamy. Add the shallot mixture, stir in the oil, add the tarragon and tomatoes and mix all the ingredients together. Season with salt and cayenne pepper. Heat carefully but do not bring to the boil.

❺ Put the ravioli and asparagus in a large bowl or arrange on large plates and pour the sauce on top.

Serves 4. About 462 kcal per serving

Gnocchi with tomatoes and sage

Gnocchi are Italian potato dumplings made with boiled potatoes, egg yolks and flour. They only take a few minutes to cook in boiling water and are delicious served with a tomato sauce.

1 Boil the potatoes, unpeeled, for 20–25 minutes until soft.

2 Cut the tomatoes into quarters, remove the seeds and dice. Peel the shallots and chop finely.

3 Heat the oil in a pan. Add the chopped shallots and sweat until transparent. Now add the diced tomatoes, stir and season with salt and pepper. Simmer the tomato mixture on a medium heat for about 10 minutes until the tomatoes are cooked. Taste and adjust the seasoning if necessary.

4 Bring about 2 litres/3 1/2 pints (9 cups) salted water to the boil in a large saucepan.

5 Peel the potatoes while they are still hot and put them on a plate. Mash them thoroughly with a fork. Add the egg yolks, salt and flour and knead into the mashed potatoes until the mixture is smooth. Using a teaspoon, take small amounts of this potato and flour dough and shape into small balls, rolling each one between the palms of your hand. Flatten the gnocchi slightly with a fork and cook them a few at a time in boiling water for about 4 minutes. Remove with a perforated spoon.

6 Melt the butter in a saucepan and fry the sage briefly. Toss the gnocchi in the butter and sage and put on individual plates. Serve with tomato sauce and Pecorino cheese.

Serves 4. About 539 kcal per serving

1 kg/2 1/4 lb potatoes, cooked floury

1 kg/2 1/4 lb ripe medium tomatoes

2 shallots

2 tablespoons sunflower oil

salt

pepper

3 egg yolks

200 g/7 oz (2 cups) flour

15 g/1/2 oz (1 tablespoon) butter

12 leaves of sage

50 g/2 oz (1/2 cup) grated Pecorino

Ravioli with tomatoes

1 can chopped tomatoes with juice (800 g/1 3/4 lb)

1 onion

1 clove garlic

4 tablespoons olive oil

1 sprig rosemary

salt

freshly ground pepper

3 tablespoons pine nuts

800 g/1 3/4 lb fresh ravioli (with spinach filling)

Ravioli, the small squares of pasta stuffed with cheese or spinach, can be bought ready-made. Tortellini are similar, shaped like small pasta rounds, containing similar fillings to those used in ravioli.

❶ Drain the tomatoes in a colander and catch the juice in a bowl. Coarsely chop the tomatoes. Peel the onions and garlic; chop finely.

❷ Heat the olive oil in a saucepan, add the onion and garlic and fry for about 3 minutes. Next add the tomato pulp, tomato juice and rosemary. Simmer the vegetables for about 20 minutes without a lid. Season with salt and pepper.

❸ Fry the pine nuts in an ungreased pan until golden brown. Cook the ravioli in plenty of salted water, following the instructions on the packet. Pour away the water and drain thoroughly.

❹ Season the tomato sauce with salt and pepper; put the ravioli in a bowl and add the tomato sauce. Stir well. Sprinkle with pine nuts before serving

Serves 4. About 825 kcal per serving

Tagliatelle with asparagus and broccoli

250 g/9 oz white asparagus

400 g/14 oz broccoli

2 cloves garlic

50 g/2 oz (4 tablespoons) butter

salt

freshly ground pepper

250 g/9 oz mascarpone

250 g/9 oz tagliatelle

Tagliatelle is made in various colours. The creamy-coloured kind is best to combine with asparagus and broccoli.

❶ Peel the asparagus, remove the woody ends and cut into pieces 2 cm/3/4 in long. Clean and wash the broccoli and separate the florets. Peel the cloves of garlic and chop finely. Add to the broccoli and asparagus and braise lightly in the butter. Cover and cook over a low heat for 4 minutes. Season with salt and butter. Add the mascarpone, stir well and cook until the sauce becomes creamy.

❷ Cook the tagliatelle "al dente" in 2–3 litres/3 1/2–5 pints (9–13 cups) of boiling water. Pour away the water and drain. Arrange the tagliatelle on plates and garnish with the vegetables.

Serves 4. About 609 kcal per serving

Asparagus risotto

A good risotto requires patience. You can only add a small of water at a time and then you have to wait until it has been completely absorbed until adding more.

6 sticks green asparagus

6 sticks white asparagus

salt

1 teaspoon butter

1 pinch sugar

2 tablespoons cream

1 onion

2 tablespoons oil

200 g/7 oz (1 cup) risotto rice

100 ml/3 1/2 oz (scant 1/2 cup) dry white wine

freshly ground white pepper

100 g/3 1/2 oz (1 cup) grated Parmesan

chives for garnish

❶ Wash the green asparagus, peel the white asparagus and remove the woody ends. Cook the white asparagus for 15 minutes and the green asparagus for 10 minutes in salted water with butter and a pinch of sugar. Remove from the water and drain. Cut the tips off the asparagus, and cut the rest of the stalks (stems) into pieces 1 cm/3/8 in long. Purée one-third of the asparagus pieces with cream.

❷ Chop the onion finely, braise in the hot oil, add the rice and fry until golden yellow. Mix 750 ml/1 1/4 pints (3 1/4 cups) asparagus stock (broth) with the white wine. Pour onto the rice little by little, stirring constantly, until all the liquid has been absorbed. Season the risotto with salt and pepper, stir in the asparagus purée and asparagus pieces, add the Parmesan and stir well. Garnish with chives.

Serves 4. About 360 kcal per serving

Tomato risotto

This tomato risotto is an ideal "Primo Piatto" in Italy. For a more seasoned risotto, the vegetable stock (broth) can be replaced with dry white wine.

1 can chopped tomatoes
  (400 g/14 oz)

2 small onions

2 cloves garlic

2 tablespoons olive oil

120 g/5 oz (3⁄4 cup) risotto rice

350 ml/12 fl oz (1 1⁄2 cups) tomato juice

150 ml/5 fl oz (5⁄8 cup) vegetable stock (broth)

sugar

salt

pepper

50 g/2 oz (1⁄2 cup) grated Parmesan

parsley

❶ Drain the tomatoes. Peel the onions and garlic and chop finely. Heat the oil in a large saucepan, add the chopped onion and garlic and fry a little to soften. Add the risotto rice and stir well, using a wooden spoon. Fry briefly.

❷ Little by little add the tomato juice and then the vegetable stock (broth) to the risotto, stirring all the time, while the risotto cooks on a low heat for 20 minutes. Add some water if the risotto needs more liquid.

❸ When the risotto is ready, add the chopped tomatoes. Stir and heat up the risotto again. Season with sugar, salt and pepper. Sprinkle with Parmesan and parsley just before serving

Serves 4. About 252 kcal per serving

Curry risotto with apple

This dish is an example of fusion cuisine. Ingredients from more than one culture are combined to create delicious new taste sensations. In this recipe,the use of orange juice, curry and apples transform a traditional rice dish into a savoury, southern speciality with oriental overtones.

20 g/3⁄4 oz margarine

2 onions

250 g/8 oz risotto rice

2 tablespoons curry powder

500 ml/17 fl oz (2 1⁄4 cups) broth

500 g/1 lb apples

2 tablespoons lemon juice

100 ml/3 1⁄2 fl oz (scant 1⁄2 cup) orange juice

1 bunch chervil

❶ Melt the margarine in a saucepan. Peel the onions, cut into rings and sweat in the margarine until transparent.

❷ Add the rice to the onions and stir until coated. Sauté. Sprinkle over the curry powder, pour in the broth and let everything simmer with the lid on for 15 minutes.

❸ Wash the apples, remove the cores and quarter. Cut the quarters into julienne sticks and put in a bowl. Pour over the lemon and orange juice and stir. Add the apples to the rice and cook over a gentle heat for 5 to 6 minutes.

❹ Wash the chervil, pluck off the leaves and chop finely. Serve the curry risotto onto plates and garnish with the chopped chervil.

Serves 4. About 270 kcal per serving

Rice with pumpkin and mango

An deliciously sweet and spicy dish which is also very nourishing. The mild taste of the pumpkin and fruitiness of the mango combine beautifully with the rice.

❶ Wash the rice. Heat the vegetable stock (broth), add the rice and saffron, cover and simmer over a low heat for about 35–40 minutes. Add more vegetable stock (broth) if necessary – there must always be a little liquid in the pan.

❷ Peel the pumpkin, remove the seeds and soft fibres and cut into cubes. Heat the oil in a pan and fry the diced pumpkin for a few minutes. Season with lime juice, pepper and chilli powder.

❸ Peel the mango, cut into bite-sized pieces and add to the braised pumpkin. Arrange the rice and pumpkin and mango mixture on two plates and sprinkle with chopped almonds.

Serves 2. About 340 kcal per serving

100 g/3 1/2 oz long-grain rice

400 ml/14 fl oz (1 3/4 cups) vegetable stock (broth)

1 pinch saffron

300 g/10 oz pumpkin

1 tablespoon sunflower oil

1 teaspoon lime juice

freshly ground pepper

some chilli pepper

1/2 mango

1 tablespoon chopped almonds

Spelt grain risotto

These spelt grains have a particularly nutty flavour. The relatively long cooking time of about 50 minutes can be reduced to 10 minutes if you soak the spelt grains overnight.

❶ Soak the spelt grains overnight in a bowl of water.

❷ Drain the spelt grains thoroughly. Peel the shallots and chop finely. Peel the carrots and cut into thin sticks. Wash and prepare the chillies, cut lengthways, remove the seeds and cut into fine strips.

❸ Heat the olive oil in a large pan and fry the shallots until transparent. Add the spelt grains and fry briefly while stirring. Add the vegetable stock (broth), carrots and chilli. Cover and simmer over a low heat for about 10–15 minutes.

❹ Because the spelt swells up as it absorbs the liquid, it may be necessary to add more liquid. If there is too much liquid left at the end, it can be reduced by boiling it briskly over a high heat without a lid.

❺ Chop the parsley leaves finely and put in the pan. Season the spelt risotto with freshly ground pepper, salt and lemon zest.

150 g/5 oz dried unripe spelt grains

2 shallots

4 carrots

1 chilli pepper

1 teaspoon olive oil

400 ml/14 fl oz (1 3/4 cups) vegetable stock (broth)

1 bunch parsley

grated zest of 1 untreated lemon

freshly ground pepper

sea salt

Serves 2. About 315 kcal per serving

Indian vegetable curry with almond rice

Lightly fried vegetables served with rice, flavoured with Indian herbs – a culinary and visual delight! Turmeric is one of the main spices used in the preparation of curry powder. It gives food an intense yellow colour and stimulates digestion.

❶ Cover the apricots with water and bring to the boil. Cover the pan and simmer over a low heat for about 10 minutes. Drain and reserve the cooking liquid. Top up the cooking liquid with water to make 250 ml/8 fl oz (1 cup) of liquid. Add the turmeric, rice, cinnamon and cardamom. Season with salt, cover and simmer over a low heat for 15 minutes. The liquid should be completely absorbed at the end of the cooking time.

❷ Fry the flaked almonds in a non-stick pan without oil until golden yellow. Peel the carrots and cut into slices. Wash and prepare the peppers and cut into thin strips. Wash and prepare the spring onions (scallions) and cut diagonally into rings.

❸ Heat the oil in a pan, add the cumin and coriander and fry briefly. Add the carrots and braise for another 5 minutes. Add the peppers, cover and cook for 5 more minutes. Add the spring onions (scallions) and cook for another 2 minutes. Add the vegetable stock (broth), bring to the boil and season with salt and cayenne pepper.

❹ Dice the apricots. Add to the rice together with the flaked almonds. Chop the mint leaves finely and sprinkle over the vegetables. Arrange the rice and vegetables on two warmed plates.

Serves 2. About 440 kcal per serving

60 g/2 oz dried apricots

1/2 teaspoon turmeric

125 g/4 1/2 oz easy-cook long-grain rice

1 piece cinnamon stick

1 cardamom seed

sea salt

2 tablespoons flaked (slivered) almonds

3 carrots

1/2 each red, green and yellow sweet peppers

3 spring onions (scallions)

1 teaspoon groundnut oil

1/2 teaspoon cumin

1/2 teaspoon ground coriander

125 ml/4 fl oz (1/2 cup) vegetable stock (broth)

cayenne pepper

1 tablespoon fresh mint leaves

Rice pudding with apples

This is a sweet pudding for everyone with a sweet tooth, and it is particularly popular with children; then you should use apple juice in stead of white wine. It can be served with apple sauce or another stewed fruit. Another variation is to include a layer of apple sauce in the pudding itself.

❶ Heat the milk in a saucepan and melt 25 g/1 oz (2 tablespoons) of butter in it. Add the pudding rice. Cook until the rice is done, remove it from the heat and let the rice cool.

❷ Peel the apples, cut in half and remove the cores. Heat 1 litre/1 3/4 pints (4 1/2 cups) of water in a large saucepan, add the apple halves, white wine, 100 g/3 1/2 oz (1/2 cup) of sugar and the lemon juice. Simmer until soft. Remove from the pan and drain well.

❸ Cut the lemon peel finely. Separate the eggs. Cream 125 g/5 oz (5/8 cup) butter in a mixing bowl, add the egg yolks, the rest of the sugar, rum, lemon peel, cooked rice and a pinch of salt. Beat the egg whites until they stand up in peaks and fold into the rice and egg mixture.

❹ Pre-heat oven to 180°C (350°F), Gas Mark 4.

❺ Grease an ovenproof dish. Spoon in half of the egg and rice mixture and cover with the apples. Add the remaining rice. Sprinkle the sugar, cinnamon and butter in flakes over the top and bake in the oven for 1 hour. Test with a skewer to see if it is done.

Serves 4. About 1250 kcal per serving

350 ml/12 fl oz (1 1⁄2 cups) milk

150 g/6 oz (3⁄4 cup) butter

375 g/13 oz (1 3⁄4 cups) pudding rice

2 kg apples

150 ml/5 fl oz (5⁄8 cup) white wine

125 g/4 oz (generous 1⁄2 cup) sugar

juice and peel from 1/2 unsprayed lemon

5 eggs

2 tablespoons rum

salt

softened margarine for the dish

1 teaspoon coarse sugar

cinnamon

butter for the top

Stuffed tomatoes with rice and sultanas (golden raisins)

These tomatoes stuffed with rice and sultanas (golden raisins) and other tasty ingredients including almonds, curry powder and cinnamon are delicious with most vegetable dishes.

❶ Peel and chop the shallots. Cut the tops off the tomatoes and carefully remove the tomato pulp using a teaspoon.

❷ Chop the tomato pulp finely and put in a bowl. Add the uncooked rice, chopped shallots, chopped almonds and sultanas (golden raisins). Stir well and sprinkle lightly with cinnamon and curry powder. Season with salt and pepper. Stir thoroughly again.

❸ Put the hollowed-out tomatoes next to each other in a large saucepan and fill with the tomato and rice stuffing. Mix the oil and tomato ketchup and pour over the tomatoes. Carefully fill the saucepan with water to reach halfway up the tomatoes.

❹ Cover the saucepan, bring to the boil and simmer gently for about 30 minutes. Remove the stuffed tomatoes from the saucepan with a perforated spoon.

Serves 4. About 404 kcal per serving

2 shallots

8 beef tomatoes

150 g/5 oz (3/4 cup) rice

2 teaspoons chopped almonds

50 g/2 oz (1/3 cup) sultanas (golden raisins)

ground cinnamon

curry powder

salt

pepper

4 tablespoons tomato ketchup

8 tablespoons sunflower oil

Sauces, dips & preserves

yolks of 4 eggs
2 teaspoons lemon juice
salt
freshly ground white pepper
250 g/9 oz (1 1/4 cups) butter

Hollandaise sauce

The eggs must be taken out of the refrigerator at least 2 hours before using so that they are at room temperature.

Stir the egg yolks and lemon together, season with salt and pepper and whisk vigorously to obtain a creamy texture. Put in a bain-marie and stir over simmering water until it has thickened sufficiently. Add warm, melted butter little by little, whisking all the time.

Serves 4. About 535 kcal per serving

ingredients for hollandaise sauce (see above)
In addition:
80 g/3 oz (6 tablespoons) butter
60 g/2 1/2 oz (1/2 cup) walnuts

Walnut hollandaise sauce

This is a delicious and easy variation on hollandaise sauce, simply made by the addition of finely chopped walnuts.

❶ Make hollandaise sauce as shown in the recipe above.

❷ Cut the butter into pieces and whisk into the sauce little by little. Chop the walnuts finely and stir into the sauce.

Serves 4. About 382 kcal per serving

Cheese sauce

This cheese sauce acquires an exquisite asparagus aroma if asparagus stock (broth) is used instead of water.

1 Heat the water, make the sauce mix and bring to the boil. Melt the processed cheese in it and stir to obtain a smooth texture. Add the crème fraîche and season with salt, pepper and lemon juice.

2 Mix the lemon zest and Parmesan. Sprinkle on the sauce when it is served.

Serves 4. About 450 kcal per serving

1 packet light sauce mix to make 250 ml/8 fl oz (1 cup) liquid

200 g/7 oz soft cream cheese

150 g/5 1/2 oz crème fraîche

salt

freshly ground pepper

1 tablespoon lemon juice

1 tablespoon grated zest of 1 untreated lemon

5 tablespoons grated Parmesan

Paprika and yoghurt sauce

Quick and easy to prepare, this sauce adds an exotic note to any asparagus dish

Stir some cornflour (cornstarch) and paprika into a little cold stock (broth). Heat the remaining stock (broth) and cream, stir in the paprika mixture, bring to the boil and cook for 1–2 minutes, stirring constantly. Remove the sauce from the heat and stir in the yoghurt. Season with salt and pepper.

Serves 4. About 108 kcal per serving

3 teaspoons cornflour (cornstarch)

2 teaspoons paprika

200 ml/7 fl oz (7/8 cup) vegetable stock (broth)

100 ml/3 1/2 oz (scant 1/2 cup) cream

150 g/5 1/2 oz natural yoghurt

1 pinch salt

1 pinch sugar

Green sauce

Green sauce made from spinach and cream is particularly good with asparagus and small new potatoes, tossed in butter.

200 g/7 oz creamed spinach, frozen

2 onions

25 g/1 oz (2 tablespoons) butter

200 g/7 oz crème fraîche

salt

freshly ground pepper

❶ Defrost the spinach, peel the onions and chop finely.

❷ Melt the butter, add the onions and fry until transparent. Add the spinach and cook. Stir in the crème fraîche. Season with salt and pepper.

Serves 4. About 300 kcal per serving

Avocado sauce

Naturally avocado sauce can also be made with home-made hollandaise. For the hollandaise sauce, see recipe p. 168.

275 ml/9 fl oz (1 1/8 cup) milk

1 small container hollandaise sauce of about 60 ml/2 fl oz (6 tablespoons)

2 avocados

juice of 1 lemon

1 pinch sugar

freshly ground pepper

❶ Heat up the milk, stir in the hollandaise sauce and bring to the boil.

❷ Halve the avocados, remove the stones (seeds) and scoop out the pulp with a spoon, mash and sprinkle with lemon juice.

❸ Stir the avocado purée into the hollandaise sauce and season with sugar and pepper.

Serves 4. About 275 kcal per serving

Vodka cherry tomatoes

This will add a Russian note to your dinner party. It is a perfect way of refreshing the palate between courses.

❶ Prick the cherry tomatoes all over with toothpick. Remove the peppercorns from the brine and crush with the back of the knife. Reserve the brine.

❷ Pour the vodka into a dish, add the brine and pepper. Put the cherry tomatoes in it next to each other. Cover with cling film and leave in the refrigerator for 2 hours.

❸ Put the herb salt and white pepper in a bowl, mix well and serve as a dip for the cherry tomatoes. Cut the lemon into eight pieces and garnish the herb salt with them. Drain the cherry tomatoes before serving.

Makes 4 jars. About 83 kcal per jar

500 g/18 oz cherry tomatoes

2 small containers pickled, green peppercorns

1 cup vodka

4 tablespoons herb salt

1 tablespoon white pepper from the mill

1 lemon

Herb sauce

1 teaspoon mustard

125 g/4 1/2 oz low fat milk
  yoghurt

1 tablespoon lemon juice

salt

freshly ground pepper

2 tablespoons chopped herbs:
  parsley, chives, chervil, dill,
  green coriander (cilantro)

100 ml/3 1/2 oz (scant 1/2 cup)
  cream

The herbs used to flavour this sauce can be varied according to taste or depending on what is available in your herb garden.

❶ Stir the mustard, yoghurt and lemon juice together to make a smooth sauce. Season with salt and pepper and add the herbs.

❷ Whip the cream until thick and stir into the herb sauce.

Serves 4. About 78 kcal per serving

Tarragon sauce

2 eggs

juice of 1 lemon

450 ml/16 fl oz (2 cups) cream

4 teaspoons mustard, medium
  strong

4 tablespoons tarragon vinegar

2 bunches tarragon

olive oil

salt

freshly ground pepper

The appearance and taste of this sauce can be altered by adding 2–3 peeled, chopped tomatoes to it.

Stir the eggs, lemon, cream, mustard and tarragon vinegar together. Add the finely chopped tarragon and olive oil. Season with salt and pepper.

Serves 4. About 350 kcal per serving

Tomato and honey sauce

This sweet, spicy sauce can be used to accompany a wide variety of dishes. It is delicious served hot with rice, braised broccoli or potato cakes.

❶ Peel the onion and garlic clove. Chop both finely. Peel the tomatoes, cut into quarters and remove the seeds. Cut the tomato quarters into small cubes.

❷ Heat the oil in a pan. Add the onion with the garlic and fry. Add the diced tomatoes, honey, vinegar, salt and pepper and stir well. Cook the sauce until it thickens, stirring constantly.

❸ Season the tomato and honey sauce with salt and pepper according to taste. Serve hot or cold.

Serves 4. About 126 kcal per serving

1 small onion

1 clove garlic

8 medium tomatoes

3 tablespoons basil-infused oil

2 tablespoons forest honey

1 tablespoon balsamic vinegar

salt

pepper

Traditional tomato sauce for pasta

Spaghetti with tomato sauce has become a classic which is always popular with everyone, whether as a first or main course. It is a good idea to prepare large amounts of the sauce in advance and freeze in individual portions. This makes it possible to conjure up a delicious meal in no time at all. The sauce is simply defrosted, and reheated while the pasta is cooked.

❶ Peel the tomatoes, cut into quarters and remove the seeds. Chop the tomatoes into small cubes. Peel the shallots and clove of garlic and chop finely.

❷ Heat the oil in a pan. Add the shallots and garlic and fry them. Then add the diced tomatoes and season with salt, pepper, sugar and vinegar. Bring to the boil and simmer for about 45 minutes over a low heat with the lid on. If the sauce becomes too thick, add a little water.

❸ Continue simmering the sauce for another 5 minutes. Season again to taste. Serve hot.

Serves 4. About 87 kcal per serving

800 g/1 3⁄4 lb beef tomatoes

2 shallots

1 clove garlic

2 tablespoons olive oil

salt

pepper

1 pinch sugar

1 tablespoon balsamic vinegar

Cheese dip

Stir all the ingredients together and season with the condiments listed.

Serves 4. About 324 kcal per serving

200 g/7 oz cream curd cheese

225 ml/8 fl oz (1 cup) cream

salt

freshly ground pepper

1 teaspoon parsley, finely chopped

1 teaspoon chervil, finely chopped

1 teaspoon lemon balm, finely chopped

Tomato dip

Stir all the ingredients together and season with the condiments listed.

Serves 4. About 64 kcal per serving

70 g//2 1/2 oz tomato purée

3 tablespoons crème fraîche

juice of 1/2 lemon

salt

freshly ground pepper

1 pinch sugar

Orange dip

Stir all the ingredients together and season with the condiments listed.

Serves 4. About 100 kcal per serving

125 ml/4 fl oz (1/2 cup) double (heavy) cream, whipped

3 tablespoons orange juice

1/2 teaspoon sugar

1 pinch salt

ginger, ground

Cherry tomatoes preserved with olives and sheep's milk cheese

Bottled tomatoes are an ideal nibble to serve with an aperitif of still or sparkling wine. They can be served in small bowls and eaten with a fork.

❶ Prick the tomatoes all over with a toothpick. Cut up the sheep's milk cheese into cubes of 2 cm/3/4 in.

❷ Coarsely chop the parsley, peel the garlic and slice into thin shavings. Fill a large jar of 1.5 litres/2 3/4 pints (7 cups) with alternate layers of sheep's milk cheese, tomatoes, olives, garlic and herbs.

❸ To make the marinade: mix the oil and vinegar and season with salt, pepper and sugar. Pour the marinade into the preserving jar to cover all the ingredients.

❹ Cover the jar with cling film and leave in the fridge to marinate for one day. Store in a cool place. Use within four days.

Serves 4. About 402 kcal per serving

500 g/18 oz cherry tomatoes

500 g/18 oz sheep's milk cheese

1 bunch smooth parsley

1 clove garlic

60 g/2 oz black olives, stoned (pitted)

60 g/2 oz green olives, stoned (pitted)

150 ml/5 fl oz (5⁄8 cup) wine vinegar

500 ml/17 fl oz (2 1/4 cups) olive oil

salt

coloured pepper from the mill

sugar

Tomato and avocado salsa

This salsa dip is made from tomatoes and avocado is a spicy dip for Mexican tortilla chips. It is also a tasty spread which is delicious on bread.

❶ Peel the tomatoes, cut into quarters and remove the seeds. Cut the tomato quarters into very small cubes. Peel the shallots and the garlic clove; chop finely. Coarsely chop the parsley. Cut the avocados in half lengthways, remove the stone (pit) and scoop out the flesh with a spoon; cut the avocado into small cubes.

❷ Mix all these ingredients together and season with chilli powder and lime juice. Stir the crème fraîche until smooth and add to salsa.

Serves 4. About 131 kcal per serving

400 g/14 oz plum tomatoes

2 shallots

1 clove garlic

1/2 bunch smooth parsley

1 avocado

salt

1/4 teaspoon chilli powder

juice of 1 lime

2 tablespoons crème fraîche

Devil's dip

This cold dip is a wonderful complement to sandwiches. You can adjust how hot and spicy it is by using more or less pepper. This sauce also goes well with vegetables.

❶ Peel, quarter and core the apples. Cut the quarters into fine julienne strips.

❷ Put the apples in a bowl and add the tomato ketchup (catsup), mustard, mayonnaise and lemon juice. Stir well.

❸ Season with salt and pepper. Wash the chives, snip into little round sections and stir in. Serve the sauce hot or cold.

Serves 4. About 110 kcal per serving

100 g/3 1/2 oz apples

100 g/3 1/2 oz (scant 1/2 cup) tomato ketchup (catsup)

20 g/3/4 oz (2 tablespoons) mustard

40 g/1 1/2 oz (4 tablespoons) mayonnaise

juice of 1/2 lemon

salt

freshly ground black pepper

1/2 bunch chives

Pear and tomato chutney sauce

Pears and tomatoes make an excellent sweet-and-sour chutney sauce. It is a particularly good relish with savoury puff pastry rolls such as spring rolls, or with deep-fried vegetables.

❶ Drain the pears and dice them. Cut the tomatoes into quarters, remove the seeds and cut into thin strips. Sprinkle a little salt on the tomato strips. Peel the onions and cut into rings.

❷ Put the diced pears, tomato strips and onion rings in a saucepan, add vinegar and bring to the boil. Season with powdered mustard, pepper, sugar, salt and cinnamon sticks. Cook the mixture until thick, stirring repeatedly.

❸ Remove the cinnamon sticks after cooking and pour the chutney into preserving jars. Store in a refrigerator. Use within 1 week of opening.

Serves 4. About 320 kcal per serving

1 can pears (400 g/14 oz)

300 g/10 oz beef tomatoes

3 small red onions

250 ml/8 fl oz (1 cup) apple vinegar

1 teaspoon mustard powder

1/2 teaspoon white pepper

200 g/7 oz brown sugar

salt

1 cinnamon stick

Desserts

Banana dessert

A healthy diet can also include puddings! This is clearly demonstrated by this mouthwatering banana pudding which is light, easy to digest and contains no fat.

❶ Peel the banana and cut in half lengthways. Sprinkle with lemon juice. Pour some honey on a plate and roll the bananas in it so that they are well coated.

❷ Put the oats in a non-stick pan and fry until light brown without adding any fat. Lay the banana halves on the roasted oats and fry for a few minutes on the flat side first. Then turn the banana over very carefully so that the oats do not fall off and fry the other side.

❸ Place the hot bananas on two plates and sprinkle the remaining fried oats on top. Serve immediately.

Serves 2. About 120 kcal per serving

1 banana
1 teaspoon lemon juice
2 teaspoons honey
2 tablespoons oat flakes

Baked pineapple

Pineapple on its own can be eaten in large amounts because it contains a large amount of cleansing substances. But served as dessert, two slices will be enough because the added sugar or honey is turned into fat by the body.

❶ Cut the pineapple slices in half, place on a baking sheet covered with aluminium foil and sprinkle rum and acacia honey over them.

❷ Pre-heat the oven to 180°C (350°F), Gas mark 4.

❸ Bake the pineapple in the oven for about 5–8 minutes. Arrange the pineapple pieces on two large plates and sprinkle with coconut milk while still hot.

Serves 2. About 130 kcal per serving

4 slices fresh pineapple
   (about 1 cm/3⁄8 in thick)
2 tablespoons acacia honey
2 teaspoons white rum
2 teaspoons coconut milk

Honey pancakes (crepes)

Sweet pancakes (crepes) can also be low in fat: but it is important to cook them in a non-stick pan so that no oil is needed. The only oil will be in the batter.

❶ Put the spelt flour, buttermilk and thistle oil in a bowl and stir to make a smooth mixture.

❷ Add the two eggs one after the other and beat the batter vigorously. Add the salt and vanilla sugar and stir. Leave the batter to stand for 25 minutes at least and stir again before the next stage.

❸ Heat a non-stick pan and pour in about a quarter of the batter. Cook each pancake (crepe) over a low heat for 2 minutes on each side until golden yellow. Take out of the pan and keep warm.

❹ Spread some honey on the pancakes (crepes) while they are still warm and sprinkle cinnamon according to taste. Roll them up and sprinkle with icing (confectioner's) sugar.

Serves 2. About 250 kcal per serving

60 g/2 oz (1/2 cup) spelt flour

100 ml/3 1/2 fl oz (1/2 cup) buttermilk

1 teaspoon thistle oil

2 eggs

1 pinch salt

1/2 teaspoon vanilla sugar

about 2 tablespoons honey

some cinnamon

icing (confectioner's) sugar

Gooseberry soup

There are white, green, red and yellow varieties of gooseberry. This soup can be served warm or cold. It is perfect as an elegant starter for an Asian menu.

1 Wash the gooseberries, remove the stalks and the little hairs.

2 Put the sugar in a heavy pan and allow to caramelize until it is light brown. Add the gooseberries and pour the wine and apple juice over them. Stir in the curry powder and simmer covered for 10 minutes.

3 Wash the lemon balm, chop the leaves from two of the sprigs and add to the soup. Blend the soup and pass through a sieve.

4 Serve garnished with the remaining leaves of lemon balm.

Serves 4. About 340 kcal per serving

500 g/1 lb gooseberries

150 g/5 oz (2/3 cup) sugar

250 ml/8 fl oz (1 cup) white wine

250 ml/8 fl oz (1 cup) unfiltered apple juice

1 pinch curry powder

4 sprigs lemon balm

Apple in mulled wine

A delicious winter dessert with an exquisite aroma of cloves and cinnamon which is very easy to prepare.

1 Bring 125 ml/4 fl oz (1/2 cup) water to the boil in a small saucepan. Add the mulled wine spices and the red wine and simmer over a low heat for about 10 minutes for the flavour to develop. Remove the sachets of spices.

2 Peel and core the apples and add whole to the wine mixture. Cover and simmer the apples over a low heat for about 15 minutes.

3 Arrange the braised apples on two plates, add the maple syrup to the mulled wine and reduce briefly over a high heat. Pour the sauce over the apples and serve immediately.

Serves 2. About 145 kcal per serving

2 sachets mulled wine spices (including cinnamon and cloves)

125 ml/4 fl oz (1/2 cup) red wine

2 apples

2 teaspoons maple syrup

Figs in red wine and blackberry sauce

A deliciously fruity pudding inspired by Mediterranean cuisine and a perfect conclusion to a light meal.

1 Wash the blackberries and put a few aside as a garnish. Purée the rest with a hand-mixer. Rub the purée through a fine sieve into a saucepan.

2 Add the red wine and heat up slowly. Mix the starch with 1 teaspoon water and stir until smooth. Add to the fruit purée and stir in carefully, making sure that there are no lumps. Bring briefly to the boil and sweeten with a tablespoon of honey.

3 Wash and prepare the figs and cut into slices. Arrange the fruit on two dessert plates and pour the hot red wine and blackberry sauce over it. Garnish with blackberries.

Serves 2. About 124 kcal per serving

125 g/4 1/2 oz blackberries

125 ml/4 fl oz (1/2 cup) red wine

1/2 teaspoon cornflour (corn starch)

1 tablespoon honey

3 fresh figs

Raspberry sorbet

This mouth-watering raspberry sorbet is completely fat-free and it makes a perfect pudding for a warm summer's day.

100 g/3 1/2 oz raspberries

1 tablespoon lemon juice

1 tablespoon honey

125 ml/4 fl oz (1/2 cup) Prosecco

1 teaspoon raspberry liqueur

some leaves of lemon balm

❶ Wash and prepare the raspberries. Purée the fruit and rub it through a fine sieve into a small freezer-proof container.

❷ Mix the lemon juice, honey, Prosecco and raspberry liqueur together. Put the fruit purée in the freezer and leave it for 3 hours to set. During the first hour, stir with a small whisk every 15 minutes, then repeat every 30 minutes.

❸ Put the raspberry sorbet in chilled glasses, garnish with lemon balm and serve immediately.

Serves 2. About 115 kcal per serving

Mango granita

This refreshingly fruity summer pudding is a granita, a light, semifrozen pudding from Italy which can be prepared with a wide range of fruits or coffee. The refined tangy flavour is enhanced by the addition of sparkling wine.

1 ripe mango

75 ml/3 fl oz (3/8 cup) sparkling white wine

75 ml/3 fl oz (3/8 cup) orange juice

1 egg white

1 teaspoon icing (confectioner's) sugar

❶ Peel the mango, cut the flesh away from the stone (pit) and chop into small pieces.

❷ Put the pieces of fruit, sparkling wine and orange juice in a tall container and make a smooth purée using a hand-mixer.

❸ Put the puréed fruit in a flat freezer tray and put in the freezer. As soon as the fruit begins to freeze, remove the purée from the container, put it in a mixing bowl and stir briskly.

❹ Beat the egg whites into stiff peaks, add the icing (confectioner's) sugar and carefully fold into the fruit purée. Put the mixture back in the freezer compartment until the fruit purée is completely frozen.

Serves 2. About 111 kcal per serving

100 g/3 1/2 oz bilberries
(blueberries)

2 teaspoons maple syrup

1 pinch cinnamon

250 g/9 oz low-fat yoghurt
(1.5%)

Bilberry (blueberry) yoghurt

Yoghurt is an ideal base for light puddings and combines beautifully with many fruits. If guests arrive unexpectedly, this delicious dish can prepared in just a few minutes.

1 Wash the bilberries (blueberries) and put a few to one side. Put the rest in a tall container with the maple syrup and a pinch of cinnamon. Purée with a hand-held mixer.

2 Using a whisk, stir the yoghurt into the bilberry (blueberry) purée. Pour into two small bowls and garnish with the reserved bilberries (blueberries).

Serves 2. About 110 kcal per serving

500 g/1 lb plums

1 pinch of salt

1 tablespoon cornflour (corn
starch)

1 teaspoon cinnamon

1 to 2 tablespoons icing
(confectioner's) sugar

125 ml/4 fl oz (1/2 cup) yoghurt

small macaroons or ladyfingers

Plum soup

The best time for making delicious fruit soups is the autumn, when there is a glut of fresh fruit. The plums in this recipe can be replaced with bilberries (blueberries) or blackberries if desired.

1 Wash and stone (pit) the plums. Heat 1 litre/1 3/4 pints (4 1/2 cups) water in a large saucepan with a pinch of salt and cook the plums until soft.

2 Mix the cornflour (corn starch) with 1 tablespoon of cold water and beat slowly into the plums. Bring briefly to the boil and reduce the heat.

3 Add the cinnamon and sugar to the plums to taste and stir in the yoghurt. Ladle the plum soup into bowls and garnish with small macaroons or ladyfingers.

Serves 4. About 110 kcal per serving

Baked apples

Baked apples are redolent of winter evenings and Christmas. In this recipe, they are given little snowy caps of meringue. Serve them with custard or whipped cream for a delicious winter treat.

❶ Wash the apples thoroughly and cut a little 'lid' off the top of each one. Carefully remove the cores from the whole apples and hollow out a little. Mix the butter with 2 tablespoons of the caraway schnapps and 2 tablespoons of sugar and spoon into the apples.

❷ Pre-heat oven to 225°C (435°F), Gas Mark 7.

❸ Grease an oven dish with the remaining butter. Arrange the apples in it and bake for 25 minutes.

❹ Beat the egg white with the remaining sugar and the cinnamon until it forms peaks. Mix the apple sauce with the remainder of the caraway schnapps. Take the apples out of the oven. Fill with the apple sauce and spoon on the beaten egg whites.

❺ Return to the oven on the top shelf and bake until golden yellow.

Serves 4. About 250 kcal per serving

550 g/1 1/4 lb untreated apples

2 tablespoons butter

3 tablespoons caraway schnapps (such as Kümmel)

3 tablespoons sugar

1 egg white

sprinkling of cinnamon

8 tablespoons apple sauce

2 tablespoons chopped almonds

Yoghurt soup with raspberries

500 ml/1 7fl oz (2 1/4 cups) low fat yoghurt

250 g/8 oz crème fraîche

juice of 1 lemon

3 tablespoons icing (confectioner's) sugar

300 g/10 oz (2 cups) raspberries

100 ml/3 1/2 fl oz (1/2 cup) cream

several mint leaves

In summer, a sweet soup such as this chilled one with yoghurt and raspberries is particularly refreshing. You can replace the raspberries with bilberries (blueberries) or strawberries if desired. However, you should use only one kind of berry at a time.

❶ Mix the yoghurt and crème fraîche well with the lemon juice and the icing (confectioner's) sugar. Add about one-third of the raspberries and reserve the rest for garnishing.

❷ Blend the yoghurt mixture with the berries and refrigerate for 1 hour.

❸ Whip the cream. Fill cooled bowls with the yoghurt soup and decorate with the reserved raspberries. Garnish with the whipped cream and the leaves of mint.

Serves 4. About 440 kcal per serving

Rhubarb soup

500 g/1 lb rhubarb

120 g/4 oz (generous 1/2 cup) sugar

3 tablespoons raspberry syrup

zest and juice of 1/2 unsprayed lemon

2 tablespoons cornflour (corn starch)

50 g/2 oz (1/2 cup) hazelnuts (filberts)

rusks (zwieback crackers)

The sour, fruity flavour of rhubarb makes a refreshing soup that can be eaten hot or cold. Serve with rusks or toasted white bread which can be easily dipped in the soup.

❶ Wash the rhubarb, peel and cut into 2 cm/1 in pieces. Heat 1 litre/1 3/4 pints (4 1/2cups) water in a large saucepan and add the rhubarb, sugar, raspberry syrup, lemon zest and lemon juice.

❷ Cook over a gentle heat until the rhubarb is soft. Mix the cornflour (corn starch) with 2 tablespoons of cold water and beat into the hot soup. Bring briefly to the boil until the soup thickens.

❸ Serve in shallow bowls with the rusks (zwieback crackers). Chop the hazelnuts (filberts) coarsely and sprinkle on top of the soup.

Serves 4. About 260 kcal per serving

Fruit salad with lemon dressing

The fruit can be chosen according to taste and season. The lemon dressing adds a delicate sharp touch to the salad and helps prevent the fruit from going brown too quickly.

❶ Peel the banana and cut into slices, peel the apricot, halve it, remove the stone (pit) and cut into quarters. Peel the honeydew melon, remove the seeds and cut into small pieces. Peel the clementines and divide into segments. Arrange the fruit in two bowls.

❷ Make the sauce with the lemon juice, maple syrup and crème fraîche and pour over the fruit.

Serves 2. About 165 kcal per serving.

1 banana

1 apricot

1 piece honeydew melon (about 200 g/7 oz)

1 clementine

1 tablespoon lemon juice

1 tablespoon maple syrup

1 tablespoon crème fraîche

Peach gratin

This deliciously fragrant peach gratin will take about 40 minutes to prepare but the result is well worth it.

❶ Blanch the peaches briefly in hot water and peel. Cut the flesh in slices off the stone (pit). Sprinkle orange juice over the fruit.

❷ Separate the egg and beat the egg yolk with 1 tablespoon of the icing (confectioner's) sugar until foamy. Stir in the quark. Beat the egg white into stiff peaks with the rest of the icing (confectioner's) sugar and a pinch of salt. Add the stiffly beaten egg white to the quark mixture.

❸ Pre-heat the oven to 200°C (400°F), Gas mark 6.

❹ Grease a small ovenproof gratin dish with butter and arrange the peach slices in it. Sprinkle chopped almonds over them. Pour the quark mixture over all and bake in the oven for about 15 minutes. Serve hot.

Serves 2. About 255 kcal per serving.

2 peaches

1 tablespoon orange juice

1 egg

2 tablespoons icing (confectioner's) sugar

125 g/4 1/2 oz low-fat quark

1 pinch salt

1/2 teaspoon butter

1 teaspoon chopped almonds

Sesame crackers

Ideal for a nibble in between meals, these crisp little sesame crackers are quick and easy to make. They will keep several days if stored in a tin or plastic box.

1 Put the spelt flakes and wheat grains in a mixing bowl, add about 400 ml/14 fl oz (1 3⁄4 cups) water and stir to make a semi-liquid dough. Leave to stand for 1 hour.

2 Pre-heat the oven to 180°C (350°F), Gas mark 4.

3 Stir the sesame seeds and salt into the dough. Grease the baking sheet with a little oil and spread out the dough on it. Bake in the oven for about 15 minutes.

4 Remove the dough from the oven and, using a sharp knife, cut a triangular or diamond-shaped pattern in the dough.

5 Replace on the baking sheet and bake for a further 15–20 minutes until crisp. Remove from the oven, leave to cool and break into triangles or diamond shapes.

Whole baking sheet about 1195 kcal

125 g/4 1/2 oz spelt flakes
125 g/4 1/2 oz fine wheat grains
60 g/2 oz sesame seeds
1 teaspoon sea salt
1 teaspoon olive oil

Lemon jelly with mango

zest and juice of 2 untreated
  lemons

100 ml/3 1/2 fl oz (1/2 cup)
  unsweetened grapefruit juice

50 ml/1 1/2 fl oz (3 tablespoons)
  orange juice

1 teaspoon acacia honey

1/2 sachet powdered gelatine

1 mango

The refreshing sharp taste of the jelly and the fruity sweetness of the
mango make an exciting contrast. In addition, this exquisite dessert has
the advantage of containing no fat at all.

❶ Put the lemon juice and zest in a small saucepan, add the grapefruit juice,
the orange juice and the acacia honey and heat slowly.

❷ In the meantime, put the powdered gelatine in 3 tablespoons of water and
leave to soak for 10 minutes. Add the gelatine to the hot (but not boiling) fruit
juice and dissolve, stirring continuously.

❸ Remove the saucepan from the heat and let the liquid cool down a little.
Pour the lemon jelly into two glass bowls and put in the refrigerator for 3
hours.

❹ Peel the mango just before serving, cut the flesh from the stone (pit) and cut
into bite-sized pieces. Garnish the chilled jelly with the pieces of mango.

Serves 2. About 80 kcal per serving

250 ml/8 fl oz (1 cup) low-fat
  milk (1.5%)

1 teaspoon vanilla sugar

2 tablespoons round grain
  (short-grain) rice

1/2 mango

1/2 teaspoon cinnamon

1 tablespoon cornflakes

Rice pudding with mango

You need a little more time to prepare this breakfast because the rice
pudding is made just before you are going to eat it. That is why it tastes
absolutely heavenly. It is also ideal as a little snack or as a pudding.

❶ Pour the milk into a small saucepan and heat slowly. Add the rice and
vanilla sugar. Cover and simmer for about 15–20 minutes over a low heat.
You can add some milk if necessary. Remove the rice pudding from the heat
and leave to cool.

❷ Peel the mango and cut into quarters. Then cut the flesh into slices. Pour
the rice pudding into a deep bowl and garnish with the mango slices and
cinnamon. Finally, sprinkle a few cornflakes on top.

Serves 1. About 335 kcal per serving

Strawberries in bilberry (blueberry) sauce

An exquisite delicacy: fresh strawberries served in a delicious bilberry (blueberry) sauce – with no fat at all!

❶ Put the bilberries (blueberries) in a saucepan. Add the maple syrup and port. Bring to the boil while stirring and simmer over a low heat for 5 minutes until the berries burst open, resulting in a thick sauce-like mixture.

❷ Wash the strawberries, hull (shuck) and cut the fruit in half. Arrange them on two pudding plates and pour the sauce over while still hot. Sprinkle icing (confectioner's) sugar on top and garnish with mint leaves.

Serves 2. About 115 kcal per serving

125 g/4 1/2 oz (1 cup) bilberries
 (blueberries)

1 tablespoon maple syrup

2 teaspoons port

200 g/7 oz (1 1/4 cups)
 strawberries

a little icing (confectioner's)
 sugar

fresh mint leaves

Orange yoghurt ice cream

You can make this delicious ice cream yourself and reduce the calories at the same time, because yoghurt is used instead of cream. This gives the dish a delicate, slightly sharp taste.

❶ Mix the orange juice, orange zest and acacia honey. Add the yoghurt and stir thoroughly with a whisk.

❷ Pour the orange-yoghurt mixture into a freezer-proof container and put in the freezer compartment for about 3 hours.

❸ Using 2 tablespoons, arrange portions of the yoghurt ice cream on two plates. Sprinkle with grated chocolate.

Serves 2. About 95 kcal per serving

juice and grated zest of 2
 untreated oranges

1 tablespoon acacia honey

250 g/9 oz fat-free yoghurt

2 tablespoons grated chocolate

Banana omelette

A banana omelette is a delicious way of ending a light meal and it also makes a delicious sweet snack. It is best eaten as soon as it has been prepared. Naturally the omelette may also be filled with other fruit.

1 Pre-heat the oven to 180°C (350°F), Gas mark 4.

2 Separate the eggs. Put the egg yolks in a bowl and beat with half the icing (confectioner's) sugar and two tablespoons of warm water to make a pale yellow foamy mixture. Add a pinch of salt to the egg whites and beat until stiff, then add the remaining sugar.

3 Add the beaten egg whites, flour and baking powder to the egg yolk mixture and fold in carefully. Line a baking sheet with greaseproof (waxed) paper. Put 4 balls of the mixture on the paper, leaving room between them, and flatten the tops slightly. Bake the omelettes in the oven for about 10–15 minutes until light brown.

4 Sprinkle vanilla sugar on a clean tea towel and turn the hot omelettes upside down onto it. Remove the greaseproof (waxed) paper.

5 Peel the bananas and cut into slices. Mix the milk and quark and add to the banana slices. Fill the omelettes with the banana-quark mixture and serve immediately.

Serves 2. About 510 kcal per serving

2 eggs

50 g/2 oz (scant 1⁄2 cup) icing (confectioners) sugar

1 pinch salt

40 g/1 1⁄2 oz (scant 1⁄2 cup) coarse wholemeal (wholewheat) flour

1⁄2 teaspoon baking powder

2 tablespoons vanilla sugar

2 bananas

2 teaspoons low-fat quark

1 teaspoon semi-skimmed milk (1.5 %)

Elderberry soup with little yeast dumplings

Juice, syrup and fried pancakes (crepes) can be made from the dark berries of this strongly scented bush. In this recipe, the sweet, yeast dumplings turn the soup into a main course.

1 Put the sugar in a heavy pan and caramelize until light brown. Add the washed berries and pour the wine ove them. Simmer for 10 minutes. Blend the berries and pass through a sieve. Mix the cornflour (corn starch) with some water and stir until smooth. Add to the soup and briefly bring to the boil again.

2 For the dumplings, sift the flour into a bowl and make a well in the centre. Heat one-third of the milk until lukewarm. Dissolve the yeast and 20 g/1 oz (1 tablespoon) sugar in the milk and add to the flour. Turn some of the flour from the edge of the well onto the surface and leave covered in a warm place for 15 minutes.

3 Knead vigorously with the egg yolks, 20 g/1 oz (1 tablespoon) sugar, half the butter, salt and lemon zest. Make the dough into little balls and leave to rise for 30 minutes.

4 Bring the remaining milk with the butter and sugar to the boil in a large saucepan. Add the little balls of dough, leaving room between them, and cook over a low heat for 20 minutes with the lid on.

5 Dust icing (confectioner's) sugar over the finished dumplings and caramelize them briefly under the grill.

6 Ladle the soup into soup plates and add the dumplings.

Serves 4. About 440 kcal per serving

For the soup:

50 g/2 oz (1/4 cup) sugar

300 g/10 oz elderberries

100 ml/3 1/2 fl oz (1/2 cup) red wine

2 teaspoons cornflour (corn starch)

For the dumplings:

200 g/7 oz (2 cups) plain (all purpose) flour

15 g/1/2 oz (1 tablespoon) yeast

250 ml/8 fl oz (1 cup) milk

60 g/2 oz (1/4 cup) sugar

1 egg yolk

30 g/1 oz (2 tablespoons) butter

pinch of salt

zest of 1/2 unsprayed lemon

2 tablespoons icing (confectioner's) sugar

Grapefruit cream

This pudding is prepared with low-fat quark. It is the gelatine which gives the pudding its consistency, which is why the pudding must be chilled for a few hours.

❶ Halve the grapefruit and squeeze out the juice. Stir the vegetable gelatine into 3 tablespoons of grapefruit juice and leave to soak for 10 minutes.

❷ Beat the egg whites stiff and add the icing (confectioner's) sugar. Mix together the quark and crème fraîche and add the rest of the grapefruit juice. Heat the gelatine until it is completely dissolved, stirring continuously. Leave to cool slightly and add to the quark mixture.

❸ Finally, fold in the stiffly beaten eggs. Put the grapefruit cream in two bowls and put in the refrigerator for about 3 hours.

Serves 2. About 235 kcal per serving

1 pink grapefruit

1 teaspoon Agar Agar

2 egg whites

3 tablespoons icing (confectioner's) sugar

200 g/7 oz low-fat quark

1 tablespoon crème fraÎche

Quark delight with almonds

The fried almonds give this quark pudding a delicate nutty flavour. In order to keep the calories down, it is important to use low-fat quark and unsweetened fruit.

❶ Mix together the milk and maple syrup. Put the quark into two pudding bowls.

❷ Peel the nectarines, cut in half, remove the stone (pit) and cut into slices. Arrange the nectarine slices on the quark.

❸ Coarsely chop the almonds, fry in a pan without fat and sprinkle over the quark and nectarine slices.

Serves 2. About 215 kcal per serving

250 g/9 oz low-fat quark

2 tablespoons low-fat milk (1.5%)

1 tablespoon maple syrup

2 nectarines

1 tablespoon almonds

Melon and orange salad

Melons contain a lot of water and very little fructose, which makes them ideal as a refreshing dessert. They make a delicious fruit salad when combined with oranges.

❶ Peel the watermelon, remove the seeds and cut the flesh into small cubes. Peel the orange and cut into segments. Cut the orange segments in half and put in a bowl with the diced melon.

❷ Mix the orange liqueur, cinnamon, honey and lemon juice together. Pour it over the fruit salad and stir well. Put in a cool place and leave to stand for about 30 minutes. Coarsely chop the walnuts and sprinkle over the melon and orange salad.

Serves 2. About 180 kcal per serving

1/4 watermelon

1 orange

1 teaspoon orange liqueur

1/2 teaspoon cinnamon

1 teaspoon honey

1 tablespoon lemon juice

1 tablespoon walnuts

Zabaglione with blackberries

Zabaglione is an Italian dessert which is made with fresh eggs and white wine. Served with blackberries, it is a light, refreshing pudding which is prepared in no time.

❶ Put the egg yolks and icing (confectioner's) sugar in a pudding bowl and whisk with an electric hand-mixer for about 5 minutes on the highest speed until the mixture has become thick and creamy.

❷ Add the Marsala and lemon juice. Heat some water in a large saucepan and keep warm over a low heat. Put the pudding bowl in the water, like a bain marie, and beat the creamy mixture until the mixture becomes very thick. Then put the bowl briefly in cold water to cool the mixture.

❸ Wash the blackberries and arrange on two plates, pour the zabaglione on top and serve immediately.

Serves 2. About 200 kcal per serving

2 fresh egg yolks

2 tablespoons icing (confectioner's) sugar

50 ml/1 1/2 fl oz (3 tablespoons) Marsala

1 teaspoon lemon juice

150 g/5 oz fresh blackberries

Tipsy apple and peach salad

It is the marzipan, honey and herb liqueur which distinguish this special fruit salad. Made with a herb liqueur which is a pure essences of herbs, your dessert will be healthy as well as delicious.

❶ Peel, quarter and core the apples. Cut into slices and put in a bowl. Sprinkle immediately with lemon juice and mix.

❷ Wash the peaches, stone and cut into thin wedges. Add to the apples in the bowl and mix carefully.

❸ Mix the marzipan with the honey, liqueur and cream. Stir into the fruit and fill small bowls with the salad. Chop the walnuts and sprinkle over the salad before serving.

Serves 4. About 430 kcal per serving

550 g/1 1/4 lb untreated apples

juice of 1 lemon

3 peaches

50 g/2 oz (4 tablespoons) marzipan

1 tablespoon honey

6 tablespoons herb liqueur

6 tablespoons cream

100 g/3 1/2 oz (1 cup) walnuts

Apple Chelsea pastries

These diminutive apple pastries are an exquisite delicacy. The dried apple rings and the pine kernels make them perfect for any occasion as well as a pleasant addition to a party buffet. Other nuts can be substituted in place of the rather expensive pine kernels if desired.

50 g/2 oz (1/3 cup) dried apple rings

3 tablespoons Calvados

100 g/3 1/2 oz (1 cup) pine kernels

200 g/7 oz (2 cups) plain (all purpose) flour

50 g/2 oz (6 tablespoons) cornflour (cornstarch)

1 egg

50 g/2 oz (1/4 cup) sugar

100 g/3 1/2 oz (1/2 cup) softened margarine

2 tablespoons apple jelly

2 tablespoons apricot jam (jelly)

❶ Pre-heat oven to 180°C (350°F), Gas Mark 4.

❷ Cut the dried apple rings into little pieces and put in a bowl. Sprinkle with Calvados and leave to marinate for 30 minutes. Spread the pine kernels on a baking tray, put in the oven and roast until golden brown.

❸ Take the pine kernels out of the oven and allow to cool. Grind half of the kernels finely and chop the rest.

❹ Mix the flour and the cornflour (cornstarch) and sift into a bowl. Add the egg, sugar, soft butter or margarine, apple pieces and the ground pine kernels. Stir everything together and mix to a smooth dough, using a whisk. Put in the refrigerator to cool briefly.

❺ Take the dough out of the refrigerator and roll out to a rectangle about 30 x 35 cm (12 x14 in). Spread the apple jelly over it and sprinkle with the chopped pine kernels. Roll up carefully and return for a short time to the refrigerator.

❻ Turn the oven up to 200°C (400°F), Gas Mark 6.

❼ Take the roll out of the refrigerator and cut into slices 1 cm/1/2 in thick. Arrange the pieces on a baking sheet covered with parchment and bake for 20 to 25 minutes.

❽ Take the rolls out of the oven and leave to cool. Heat the apricot jam (jelly) in a small pan with 2 tablespoons of water and brush over the rolls.

Makes 12 pieces. About 240 kcal per piece

Drinks

Exotic fruit drink

This fruit drink made from papaya and mango is a delicious summer drink and does not contain any fat at all. Like other fruit juices, it can also be diluted to taste with mineral water.

❶ Peel the papaya and mango, remove the stone (pit) and cut the flesh into small cubes.

❷ Cut the orange in half and squeeze the juice . Pour the orange juice, cubed papaya and mango into the liquidizer and purée.

❸ Season the fruit drink with a pinch of cinnamon, dilute to taste with mineral water and pour into a large glass.

Makes 1 glass. About 143 kcal per glass

1/2 papaya
1/2 mango
1 orange
pinch cinnamon
sparkling mineral water

Grapefruit and coconut juice

Citrus fruits are rich in vitamin C which protects the body against colds. Grapefruit juice is extremely refreshing and can be made in no time at all all the year round.

Halve the grapefruit and squeeze the juice. Mix the grapefruit juice with the juice of half a lime, sweeten with honey and sprinkle with grated coconut.

Makes 1 glass. About 115 kcal per glass

1 grapefruit
juice of 1/2 lime
1 teaspoon honey
2 tablespoons coconut milk
1 teaspoon grated coconut

Mango buttermilk

This is a sweet, fruity drink with only a very small amount of fat. You can make this delicious drink whenever you like because mangos are now available almost all year round.

1 ripe mango

1/2 banana

300 ml/10 fl oz (1 1/4 cups) buttermilk

1 teaspoon orange juice

1 pinch ground ginger

❶ Peel the mangos and banana. Remove the stone (pit) and cut the mango into slices, putting two slices aside for the garnish. Put the diced mango and banana in the liquidizer and purée.

❷ Add the puréed fruit to the buttermilk and stir well. Season with orange juice and ground ginger and pour into a large glass. Garnish with the slices of mango.

Makes 1 glass. About 310 kcal per glass

Blackcurrant and lemon kefir

Blackcurrant juice and kefir: an ideal combination and a perfect way to ward off colds during winter without piling up the calories.

Mix the blackcurrant juice, lemon juice and rosehip pulp together. Add the kefir, stir well and season with a pinch of cinnamon.

Makes 1 glass. About 205 kcal per glass

100 ml/3 1/2 fl oz (1/2 cup) blackcurrant juice

1 tablespoon lemon juice

1 tablespoon rosehip purée

200 ml/7 fl oz (7/8 cup) kefir

1 pinch cinnamon

Winter punch

You can also make steaming hot punch without fattening ingredients
such as alcohol or sugar. This punch consists of an infusion of fragrant
herbs with the addition of orange juice.

1 Heat about 300 ml/10 fl oz (1 1⁄4 cups) water in a small saucepan. Add the
cloves, cardamom and cinnamon stick. Bring briefly to the boil. Suspend the
tea bag in the saucepan, cover and simmer for about 10 minutes over a low
heat.

2 Remove the tea bag, cinnamon stick and cloves from the liquid. Add the orange and lemon juice. Heat the punch but do not boil. Sweeten with honey according to taste and serve hot.

Makes 1 glass. About 80 kcal per glass

1 cinnamon stick

3 cloves

1 pinch ground cardamom

1 tea bag mallow tea

juice of 1 orange

juice of 1 lemon

1 teaspoon honey

Carrot and orange drink

Vegetable and fruit drinks are truly invigorating and very delicious. They are full of important vitamins and minerals and contain hardly any fat. For people with little time, they can also be mixed from ready-made juices (without added sugar!), available in health food shops.

1 orange

150 ml/5 fl oz (5⁄8 cup) carrot juice

pinch cinnamon

1 teaspoon honey

1/2 teaspoon cream

❶ Peel the orange, cut in half, cut off one slice and put to one side. Squeeze the rest of the orange.

❷ Mix the orange juice with the carrot juice, stir in the cream and season with a pinch of cinnamon and honey. Pour into a large glass and garnish with the slice of orange.

Makes 1 glass. About 160 kcal per glass

Pear and banana shake

This milk shake is like a small meal in itself because the bananas and milk contain many important nutrients. It is therefore an amazing source of energy.

1 banana

1 pear

250 ml/8 fl oz (1 cup) low-fat milk (1.5%)

1 teaspoon grated chocolate

Peel the bananas and pears. Remove the core from the pear. Cut the pear and banana into pieces and purée with the milk in the liquidizer. Pour the milk shake into a large glass and sprinkle with grated chocolate.

Makes 1 glass. About 300 kcal per glass

Peach and kiwi fruit milk shake

You should choose very ripe fruit to make this milk shake. This will make it much easier when you purée them. Instead of a peach, apricot or nectarine can also be used.

1 Peel the peach and kiwi fruit, remove the peach stone (pit) and cut both fruits into eight pieces. Put in a tall container, add a pinch of vanilla sugar and a tablespoon of sour milk, and purée with a hand-held electric mixer.

2 Add the puréed fruit to the rest of the sour milk and stir well. If the milk-shake is too thick, add some more sour milk. Pour into a tall glass and sprinkle with chopped hazelnuts.

Makes 1 glass. About 265 kcal per glass.

1 peach

1 kiwi fruit

1 pinch vanilla sugar

125 ml/4 fl oz (1/2 cup) low-fat
   sour milk

some skimmed milk

1 teaspoon chopped hazelnuts

Citrus fruit cocktail

A spicy, refreshing summer drink with no fat at all made with freshly squeezed grapefruit and orange mixed with pineapple juice.

1 Mix together the freshly squeezed orange and grapefruit juice and add the pineapple juice. Season with freshly ground ginger and pour into a glass with ice cubes.

2 Cut the carambola (star fruit) into slices, make a notch in each slice and slip onto the edge of the glass as decoration.

Makes 1 glass. About 180 kcal per glass.

juice of 1 grapefruit

juice of 1 orange

200 ml/7 fl oz (7/8 cup) unsweetened pineapple juice

pinch ground ginger

ice cubes

1/2 carambola (star fruit)

Apple and bilberry (blueberry) drink

500 g/1 lb untreated apples

2 tablespoons bilberries (blueberries)

1 unsprayed lemon

juice of 1/2 lemon

Bilberries (blueberries) are full of goodness. They used to be one of the most important sources of food for the American Indians, and were thought to protect against evil spirits. The dark purplish-blue berries can sometimes be found growing in the woods in the summer and can be picked for your drink. Otherwise, frozen ones can be used all the year round.

❶ Wash the apples thoroughly and cut into quarters. Wash and pick over the bilberries (blueberries).

❷ Juice the apples and the bilberries (blueberries) in a juicer, add lemon juice to taste and pour into glasses.

❸ Wash the lemon well and cut into eighths. Put a wedge of lemon on the edge of each glass.

Makes 1 litre/1 3/4 pints (4 1/2 cups). About 10 kcal per glass

Nectarine shake with wheat germ

2 nectarines

300 ml/10 fl oz (1 1/4 cups) buttermilk

1 teaspoon maple syrup

1 tablespoon wheat germ

This milk-shake is made with buttermilk and enriched with wheat germ. As a result, it is deliciously refreshing with a slightly sour taste as well as very nourishing.

❶ Peel the nectarines, cut them in half, remove the stone (pit) and purée in the liquidizer.

❷ Add the buttermilk and stir well. Sweeten the nectarine shake with maple syrup, pour into a tall glass and sprinkle wheat germ on top.

Makes 1 glass. About 245 kcal per glass

Cinnamon and honey flavoured cocoa

200 ml/7 fl oz (7/8 cup) low-fat
   milk (1.5%)

1 teaspoon cocoa powder

1 pinch cinnamon

1 pinch ground cardamom

1 teaspoon honey

1 teaspoon chocolate flakes

It need not always be coffee or tea – cinnamon is a very pleasant alternative flavour for that time of the day when you need a lift. Also, being prepared with low-fat milk, it is very low in calories.

❶ Heat up the milk, add the cocoa powder and stir until it is dissolved. Bring the cocoa briefly to the boil.

❷ Season the cocoa with a pinch of cinnamon and cardamom and sweeten with honey to taste. Pour the hot cocoa into a mug and garnish with chocolate flakes.

Makes 1 glass. About 155 kcal per glass

Hazelnut milk drink

1 tablespoon shelled hazelnuts

100 g/31/2 oz low-fat yoghurt
   (1.5%)

200 ml/7 fl oz (7/8 cup) low-fat
   milk

1 teaspoon honey

1/2 teaspoon vanilla sugar

Nuts are relatively high in fat which is why they should be used sparingly in low-fat cuisine. But their delicate flavour still comes through, even in small amounts, especially when freshly ground.

❶ Grind the hazelnuts finely. Put in a tall container, add the yoghurt and stir vigorously with a small whisk.

❷ Sweeten the milk-shake to taste with honey and vanilla sugar.

Makes 1 glass. About 245 kcal per glass

200 g/7 oz cucumber

1 red sweet pepper

1/2 clove garlic

100 g/3 1/2 oz low-fat yoghurt (1.5%)

sparkling mineral water

sea salt

freshly ground pepper

1 teaspoon chopped dill

Cucumber and red pepper drink

It need not always be lemonade – a vegetable drink like this one is extremely refreshing and very thirst-quenching on a hot summer's day.

❶ Peel the cucumber, remove the seeds and cut into cubes. Wash the pepper, remove the stalk and seeds, and chop. Put the vegetables in the liquidizer, then rub through a fine sieve.

❷ Peel the garlic, press it through a garlic press and add to the puréed vegetables. Stir in the yoghurt – and mineral water to taste – and whisk vigorously. Season the drink with sea salt, freshly ground pepper and finely chopped dill.

Makes 1 glass. About 115 kcal per glass

Beetroot (red beet) and carrot drink

200 ml/7 fl oz (7/8 cup) beetroot (red beet) juice

200 ml/7 fl oz (7/8 cup) carrot juice

1 teaspoon sour cream

freshly ground pepper

1 small piece horseradish

a few parsley leaves

A spicy cocktail, rich in vitamins A and C, seasoned with a little grated horseradish. Carrot juice and beetroot juice are available from health food shops, but they must be unsweetened.

❶ Mix together the beetroot (red beet) juice, carrot juice and sour cream. Stir well and season with freshly ground pepper.

❷ Peel some horseradish, grate finely and add to the mixed juices. Wash the parsley, chop the leaves finely and sprinkle on the juice.

Makes 1 glass. About 120 kcal per glass

Watermelon drink

A refreshing drink, ideal for a hot summer's day. This watermelon shake contains hardly any calories and can be diluted with mineral water, or on special occasions, with Prosecco or other sparkling white wine.

❶ Peel the watermelon and remove the seeds, cut into cubes and put in a tall mixing bowl. Purée the watermelon with a hand-held electric mixer. Season with a pinch of ground ginger, a little vanilla sugar and lemon juice.

❷ Dilute the puréed melon with mineral water or Prosecco. Pour into a tall glass and garnish with mint leaves.

Makes 1 glass. About 85 kcal per glass

1 piece watermelon (about
  200 g/7 oz)

ground ginger

1/2 teaspoon vanilla sugar

1 teaspoon lemon juice

**125 ml/4 fl oz (1/2 cup) sparkling
  mineral water or Prosecco (or
  other sparkling white wine)**

a few mint leaves

Green tea drink

Green tea is an excellent thirst quencher and is much healthier than coffee or Indian tea. In Asia, green tea is believed to have medicinal properties such as lowering cholesterol levels.

❶ Bring about 250 ml/8 fl oz (1 cup) water to the boil, remove from the heat and leave to cool a little. Put two tea bags in a pre-heated teapot and pour the hot water on top, allow to draw for about 3 minutes.

❷ Season the green tea with lime juice and ground ginger. Sweeten with honey according to taste.

Makes 1 glass. About 1 kcal per glass

1 tea bag green tea

1 tea bag peppermint tea

1 teaspoon lime juice

pinch ground ginger

1 teaspoon honey

8 ice cubes

400 ml/14 fl oz (1 3/4 cups) cold
green tea

200 ml/7 oz (7/8 cup) vegetable
juice

200 ml/7 oz (7/8 cup) tomato
juice

salt

pepper

Tabasco

2 tablespoons lime juice

Ice-cold lime and tomato tea

Green tea with vegetable and tomato juice, flavoured with lime juice
and tabasco, makes a cool, refreshing, very tasty drink which is delicious not only on warm summer's days but any time of the year.

❶ Wrap ice cubes in a tea towel and crush with a hammer. Put the crushed ice
cubes in four tall drinking glasses.

❷ Mix the vegetable and tomato juice with the green tea; season with salt, pepper, tabasco and lime juice. Pour the the lime and tomato tea into the glasses
and serve immediately.

Serves 4. About 20 kcal per serving

1/2 ripe avocado

1 teaspoon lemon juice

150 ml/5 fl oz (5/8 cup) kefir

freshly ground white pepper

1 teaspoon chives

Avocado and kefir drink

A creamy mild drink, made from very healthy ingredients. Avocados are
full of healthy unsaturated fatty acids, while the slightly tangy kefir with
its lactic acid bacteria activates the body's metabolism.

❶ Scoop out the flesh of the avocado pear with a spoon. Sprinkle with lemon
juice and purée in the liquidizer.

❷ Add the kefir and stir well. Season the avocado and kefir drink with freshly
ground pepper. Pour into a glass and sprinkle the chopped chives on top.

Makes 1 glass. About 295 kcal per glass

Pepper and celery drink

You can prepare vegetable juices yourself if you have a juicer. But naturally it is quicker with ready-made juices available in health food shops. The drink is chilled with iced whey cubes which you can make yourself in the freezer.

❶ Pour the whey into an ice-cube tray and put in the freezer.

❷ Stir the celery and red pepper juice together. Season with chilli powder and a pinch of grated nutmeg.

❸ Wash the chives, pat dry and chop finely. Remove the tray with iced whey cubes, put them in a large glass, pour in the juice and sprinkle with the chopped chives.

Makes 1 glass. About 110 kcal per glass

100 ml/3 1⁄2 fl oz (1⁄2 cup) whey

200 ml/7 fl oz (7⁄8 cup) celery
 juice

100 ml/3 1⁄2 fl oz (1⁄2 cup) red
 pepper juice

1 pinch chilli pepper

grated nutmeg

1⁄2 bunch chives

Spiced tomato cocktail

Hot spices such as chilli powder have stimulating properties, so just a pinch will turn this tomato juice into quite an invigorating drink that will give you a lift between meals.

❶ Wash the tomatoes, remove the stalks, chop into pieces, purée and rub through a fine sieve.

❷ Add the chopped chives and stir in the sour milk. Season with chilli powder and lemon juice. Dilute with mineral water according to taste.

Makes 1 glass. About 55 kcal per glass

200 g/7 oz tomatoes

1 teaspoon chives

1 tablespoon low-fat sour milk

1 pinch chilli pepper

lemon juice

sparkling mineral water